CREATIVE
THINKING

CREATIVE THINKING

HOW TO
GENERATE IDEAS
AND TURN THEM
INTO SUCCESSFUL
REALITY

MICHAEL LeBOEUF

PIATKUS

First published in Great Britain in 1990 as
How to Develop and Profit from your Creative Powers
by Judy Piatkus (Publishers) Ltd of
5 Windmill Street, London W1P 1HF

First paperback edition 1994

Originally published in the United States
in 1980 as *Imagineering*

*A catalogue record for this book is available
from the British Library*

ISBN 0 7499 1351 7

Printed and bound in Great Britain by
Mackays of Chatham PLC, Chatham, Kent

ACKNOWLEDGMENTS

With special thanks to:

Peggy Tsukahira for being a super editor.

Artie and Richard Pine for their encouragement, advice and support.

Kathy Ackermann, my typist, for her patience, loyalty and excellent work.

*To the little bit
of the creator
in us all*

Contents

The real purpose of books is to
trap the mind into doing its own thinking.

—Christopher Morley

Introduction

*"Imagination is the beginning of creation. You imagine
what you desire; you will what you imagine; and at last
you create what you will."*

—George Bernard Shaw

GOOD TIMES WILL come and go, but one thing is certain. The person who knows how to create good, new ideas and turn them into realities is the one who will prosper no matter what the future brings. This book will show you how you can become that person.

It seems ironic that we use our minds mostly for storing ideas when, in fact, they have the much greater power of producing ideas—new ideas that can be turned into successful realities. Do you, like the majority of people, think of yourself as uncreative? In Chapter One we will explore numerous, common myths and injunctions that hamper creativity and show you how to overcome them.

Are you one who recognizes your creative potential but is having trouble channeling it? Chapter Two will give you some easy ways to make tough decisions and focus your creative energies.

Do you think of creativity as something that's mystical, magical and beyond the comprehension of most of us? Chapter Three will take the mystery out of it for you. You'll learn what the essence of creativity is, how to nurture and exercise your creative abilities and be given specific, action-ready techniques that will enable you to generate new ideas at will.

Are you trying to motivate your employees, family or any group to think creatively? Chapter Four explains some proven team-creativity techniques and teaches you how to apply them.

Are you aware that asking the right questions often leads to just the idea you're looking for? Chapter Five will show you how and provide you with questions you need.

Do you know how to evaluate your ideas? There aren't any surefire methods, but Chapter Six gives you some guidelines that will up your odds of picking a winner.

Is your creative ability being hampered by the everyday stresses and strains of life? Chapter Seven gives you some tips for reducing them and putting yourself in the proper frame of mind.

Do you have a dream whose realization is being prevented by numerous obstacles such as people, inexperience, money and luck? Chapters Eight and Nine will give you some strategies for clearing the barriers that stand between you and your dream come true.

Are you just too busy to pursue your dreams? Chapter Ten gives you some key ideas for managing your time.

Do you need that initial push to get you started in the path to pursuing your dreams? In Chapter Eleven, you'll learn how to conquer the put-off game, create your own enthusiasm and develop the never-say-die attitude that's essential for creative success.

In the pages of this book, I have put every valuable, practical technique I know of for generating new ideas and turning them into successful realities. And that, in a nutshell, is what I call imagineering. The term *imagineering* is a coined word adopted by the Aluminum Company of America which means "You let your imagination soar and then engineer it down to earth." I have researched the ideas of great creators such as Franklin, Einstein, Edison, Bell, Disney and others too numerous to mention. I take no credit for the originality of these ideas but I know that they work because I've used them. Hopefully, my contribution is to assemble these ideas into one book and present them in a form that you will enjoy reading and find useful.

Will this book make you more creative? That's up to you. The value of a self-help book is much like the value of a lawn mower. You can spend a tidy sum for a new mower, but it won't cut your grass unless you get behind it and push. Similarly, reading this book and forgetting about it will do little or nothing to enhance your creativity. Actively read this book by underlining key points and taking notes. Make a list of the creative ideas that apply to you and resolve to use them. This book is a tool. Use it as such.

These concepts are applicable on the job, at home, or anywhere you choose to use them. The main point is to show you how to make your creativity work for you. I can't give you any more creative ability than you have but I'll show you how to make the most of what's there. And I promise you this: You have a whole lot more than you think you do. Read on, enjoy and learn how to harness your creative potential. It's the fountainhead of success and personal fulfillment.

P.S. Proceeding with an open mind is essential.

PART I

REDESIGNING YOUR IMAGINATION FOUNDATION

1

The Creativity Gap

"There is really nothing elusive or mysterious about creativity. Anyone who can talk is able to write. Anyone who can see is able to visualize. And anyone who can think is able to have ideas."

—Stephen Baker

THE FOUNDER OF one of the world's largest and most successful hotel chains was once asked how he managed to succeed despite the handicap of only eight years of schooling. He replied, "When a man ain't got no education, he's forced to use his brains!"

A young man in search of a job applied at Macy's and was flatly told there were too many applicants ahead of him. Undaunted, he browsed through the store and telephoned the personnel director. "I want a job and I've just spent several hours in the store looking for places where I could help," he said. "I've listed ten spots where I think I could be useful right this minute. May I come up and tell you where they are?" Needless to say, he was soon a Macy trainee.

A mother constantly nagged her children about their reluctance to practice the piano. Thinking there must be a better way to motivate them, she bought a notebook and a box of colored stars. Then she set down new rules for piano practice. Each child was to practice on his own and set the timer on the kitchen stove each time he practiced. At the end of each fifteen-minute practice period, the mother pasted a star in the child's notebook. At the end of the week, the child with the most stars was given a prize. Not only did their music improve, but the children developed a sense of personal responsibility as well.

All these stories are examples of people using their creative abilities to make life better for themselves and those around them. Imagination is our most powerful mental facility and the creation of new ideas is at the very heart of all progress.

IMAGINATION—THE OIL WELLS OF YOUR MIND

The greatest minds in history have almost unanimously acknowledged the importance of imagination. Consider the views of these three:

"Imagination is more important than knowledge."
                                            —ALBERT EINSTEIN
"Imagination makes man the paragon of animals."
                                            —SHAKESPEARE
"Imagination governs the world."
                                            —DISRAELI

The history and growth of the United States is directly tied to the vision and ability of creative people. Names such as Edison, Bell, Morse, the Wright Brothers and numerous other inventors fill the pages of our history books. And we have only to read about the discoveries and inventions of Franklin or take a tour of Jefferson's Monticello to realize that many of our founding fathers had a great deal more than political vision. They were tinkerers, inventors, discoverers, doers—in short, imagineers of the first order.

The future prosperity—indeed the very survival—of the United States will depend on imagination to generate solutions to the gigantic problems we face today. Yet today there is growing concern that America is losing its creative edge. Adlai Stevenson of Illinois, chairman of the Senate subcommittee on science, technology and space, remarked, "This is a rich and resourceful country. But its spirit of adventure and invention may be drying up. Nations fail when that happens." That statement is worthy of serious thought. Are we a people who have lost our creative edge? Has our busy, stressful, urban life-style coupled with big government, big religion, big science, big business and big education lulled us into following routines rather than blazing new trails? Worse yet, has our affluence made us complacent about the need for creative thinking and acting? If there is a creativity gap (and I believe there is), how can this be? After all, aren't we the most highly educated and technically trained society in history?

One clue to the creativity gap can be found by examining our educational techniques in light of our mental facilities. For purposes of simplicity, let's divide our mental abilities into four basic functions:

1. Observe and pay attention.
2. Memorize and recall.
3. Analyze and judge.
4. Generate new ideas, foresee and visualize the non-existent.

Our educational system sees to it that we spend the first quarter of our lives developing our abilities in the first three of those functions while the fourth goes almost totally neglected. We spend countless hours reading books and paying attention to teachers and professors who lecture on everything from the alphabet to zoology. The system continually tests our ability to memorize facts and figures and regurgitate them on command. We are continually given assignments in numerous disciplines that teach us to analyze, evaluate and critique. But almost never are we given the opportunity to exercise our creative abilities. Is it any wonder that most of us think of ourselves as noncreative? We are taught what to think and how to think, but seldom, if ever, are we taught how to think up.

That great philosopher Yogi Berra once said, "You can observe a lot just by watching." Try observing the behavior of preschool-age children and you will quickly realize the immense amount of creative potential with which all of us are endowed. Curiosity coupled with a healthy imagination is typical of a normal young child. Parental statements such as "Where did she get that idea from?" and "How does he think up such impossible questions?" are common. John J. Plomp summed it up when he remarked, "You know children are growing up when they start asking questions that have answers."

As children mature and go off to school, their imagination dwindles while the other facilities develop. Why this happens we can only speculate. However, one reason is that it's simply a case of developing three mental abilities while ignoring the fourth. Creative abilities are the oil wells of our mind. We know there's a lot there, but getting it to the surface and transforming it into something useful is the problem.

TWO MINDS IN ONE

Another insight into the creativity gap has come as the result of brain research carried out by Dr. Roger Sperry and his students Michael Gazzaniga and Jerre Levy at the California Institute of Technology. In their historic split-brain experiments, they were able to surgically separate and test the thinking abilities of each half of the human brain and found that each half of the brain has its own way of thinking and its own memories. It appears that just as we have two eyes, two ears and two hands, we also have two minds. Our left brain tends to think in terms of symbols and words while our right brain thinks in terms of sensory images. We use the left brain for the likes of logic, judgment, speaking and mathematical ability, while the right brain is the source of dreaming, feelings, visualization and intuition. Remembering someone's name is a function of the left brain memory while remembering their face is a function of the memory in the right brain. Reading a book on how to improve your tennis or golf game is the job of the left brain but getting "a feel for the game" is carried out in the right brain. Thus, our two minds have a partnership in which one side handles the language and logic while the other side does things that are difficult to put into words or symbols.

The following chart summarizes some of the differences in left- and right-brain functions:

We use our left brain for:	We use our right brain for:
speaking	awareness without description
reading	seeing whole things at once
writing	recognizing similarities
analyzing	understanding analogies and metaphors

We use our left brain for:	*We use our right brain for:*
idea-linking	intuition
abstracting	insight
categorizing	gut-level feeling
logic	synthesizing
reasoning	visualizing
judgment	spatial perception
counting and mathematical ability	visual memory
verbal memory	recognizing patterns
using symbols	"feeling" our way
managing time	relating things to the present

Creative thinking requires coordinating and using *both* sides of the brain. Flashes of insight and intuition are the result of right-brain thinking but analyzing these insights must be carried out in the left brain. Research into the thought processes of highly creative people reveals them to rely heavily on the intuitive side of their brain. In his autobiography, Max Planck, the father of quantum theory, wrote that the creative scientist must have "... a vivid imagination for new ideas not generated by deduction, but by *artistically* creative imagination." Einstein and other innovators in science and mathematics relied heavily on visual thinking before transforming their thoughts into precise equations. And centuries ago Aristotle, the founder of formal logic, wrote, "It is impossible even to think without a mental picture. The same affection is involved in thinking as in drawing a diagram."

When the results of split-brain research are considered in light of our education, a frightening fact emerges. *We're developing only the left side of our brain while the right side is being suppressed and ignored.* After years of conditioning, most of us tend to think of "thinking" and "using your head" as only left-brain thinking. The intellectual who relies solely on verbal and logical abilities is incapable of creative thought because creative thinking calls for a combination of insight and intuition coupled with verbal and logical ability. Truly creative people know how to use the tools of logic and words but recognize their limitations. Unfortunately, most of our educating is done by left-brain types who, in turn, produce more left-brain types. Educational credentials and degrees are awarded to those who demonstrate the ability to use skills that are the product of left-brain thinking. And what is typically called "scholarly" research is usually little more than an exercise in verbal and/or mathematical logic that is almost totally devoid of any right-brain thinking.

It's been said that the electronic computer is the first extension of man's mind. For the first time in history, man has a tool capable of logical and abstract thinking. However, in terms of split-brain abilities, the computer is nothing more than a gigantic left brain that's capable of doing left-brain tasks millions of times faster than we can. The result is that many of the clerical and left-brain jobs in society are being computerized and this trend will undoubtedly continue. The challenge to industry, education and society is to develop right-brain thinking that will enable us to work in harmonious partnership with the giant, electronic left-brains that we have created.

POPULAR MYTHS ABOUT CREATIVITY

In their book *Give Your Child a Superior Mind*, Siegfried and Therese Engelmann wrote, "The human animal is the only one on earth so intelligent that it can actually learn to be stupid." All of us are born with a natural facility for creative thinking and problem solving. And like many other human facilities, it has to be developed. Unfortunately, much of what we learn about creativity prevents us from developing it as much as we could. All of us have been taught ideas, theories, values and concepts about creativity by various sources and much of this information is blatantly false.

The problem of not developing our creative abilities is compounded further by erroneous beliefs we harbor about creativity and our relationship to it. The following are nine commonly held, erroneous beliefs about creativity that are at best partial truths and at worst total fantasies. As you read each one, ask yourself, "Do I believe this?" If you do, think of it as one more nail that's keeping the lid on your creative potential.

Myth #1—To Be Creative Means Imagining or Doing Something Completely New

If you believe this first myth, you've struck out before you step into the batter's box. Jean Baitaillon wrote, "Really we create nothing. We merely plagiarize nature." What is totally new? Can you think of anything that is? I can't. Every idea or thing created is an extension, synthesis or duplication of previous ideas and/or things. New books are a rearrangement of old words, ideas and concepts. New paintings are a rearrangement of color, canvas and skill. New scientific breakthroughs are built on existing fundamental principles. The list could go on endlessly.

Most of our new ideas result from associating the ideas of others. You may think Einstein was a great creative genius— and he was. But it's also true that he spent a good portion of time working in a Swiss patent office. Can you think of a better place to be kept informed of the latest developments in physics at that time? None of our ideas are completely our own and nothing anyone creates is totally new.

Most of us overestimate the uniqueness aspect of creative work and as a result we immobilize ourselves from trying. The late Dale Carnegie is credited with creating ideas that have enabled millions of people to live happier, more successful and productive lives. However, Carnegie summarized his creativity this way:

> The ideas I stand for are not mine. I borrowed them from Socrates. I swiped them from Chesterfield. I stole them from Jesus. And I put them in a book. If you don't like their rules, whose would you use?

Myth #2—Only the Experts Can Create Anything Meaningful

The wide acceptance of this myth in today's world almost qualifies it as a national disease. There is no denying the fact that specialists and experts have solved many of our problems and raised our standard of living through their creative efforts. The problem with the expert myth is simply a case of a good thing being carried to extremes. The result is that people frequently rely on experts as crutches rather than assets.

One classic case of expertsmanship involves the NBC television network. Some years back they spent about $750,000 to have experts create a new logo. The experts came back with a big red and blue *N*. Later it was discovered that the Nebraska Educational Television Network had been using the identical logo for quite some time. Thus, in addition to paying the experts $750,000, NBC paid the Nebraska network $55,000 in cash and another $500,000 in used equipment in order to gain rights to the trademark. That adds up to a total cost of $1,305,000 for a logo that one of the Nebraska network employees had designed some years back for an estimated cost of less than $100.

History is filled with great innovations carried out by people with virtually no training in the endeavors where they made their mark. Eli Whitney, who invented the cotton gin, was a schoolteacher. Samuel Morse and Robert Fulton, inventors of the telegraph and steamboat, respectively, were both artists. Being a nonexpert is often a creative asset because you aren't blinded by traditional ways of viewing the problem.

Myth #3—Only a Gifted Minority of People Are Creative

This is the most unconditionally false of the creativity myths. Nearly everyone who has studied the field agrees that creativity is a normal and universally distributed human trait. Everyone possesses some creative ability.

Interestingly, although it is believed that some people have more than others, our creative productivity appears to be more in proportion to our output of mental energy than to any amount of inborn talent. It's the drive to create new ideas that seems to count most.

The universality of imaginative talent was documented numerous times during World War II. B. F. Goodrich received three thousand employee suggestions per year, and one-third of them were good enough to earn cash awards. In 1943, the ordnance department saved over fifty million dollars due to ideas thought up by rank-and-file employees. A member of New York City's transit system thought up a shell-fragment detector that saved countless lives. The message is clear. When the motivation is there, all of us can come up with good ideas.

Myth #4—Creativity Borders on Insanity

This myth is an outgrowth of stereotypes such as the mad scientist, the nutty professor or insane poets of the Edgar Allan Poe variety. Like other stereotypes, this idea doesn't stand up under objective evaluation.

Not surprisingly, psychoanalysts reject the view that creative persons must be emotionally disturbed. Rather they tend to take the opposite approach and believe that a healthy psyche is an asset to creativity. For someone to successfully utilize his ideas, he must have a strong enough self-image to believe in himself and be able to let his mind wander without fear of losing control. The creative person is the master rather than the slave of his imagination. He feels free to fantasize because he knows he can return to reality as needed.

On the other hand, psychoanalysts believe emotional disturbances tend to hinder rather than enhance creativity. Studies of emotionally disturbed persons reveal them to be unimaginative, inflexible, unoriginal and unable to respond to problems requiring new ideas. Their creative abilities appear to be frozen within them. No doubt there have been creative individuals who harbored numerous neuroses and psychoses. However, the view today is that these people were creative despite their disorders and not because of them.

Myth #5—If You Really Have Creative Ability, Someone Will Discover You and Recognize Your Talents

In his book *The Successful Promoter*, Ted Schwarz presents the following allegory:

> Fenster Freebush built a better mousetrap. It came in three finishes and seventeen decorator colors and could lure a mouse hiding anywhere within a five-mile radius of the trap. In addition, it played stereo music and, when it was not otherwise occupied, could be used as a combination beer cooler and fondue pot for parties. Freebush had 1,000 of these units made and waited for the world to beat a path to his door. Nobody came!*

The fact that you have creative talent and ability means nothing if you don't do something with it. And one sure way to ensure wasting your talents is to wait to be discovered.

Women are particular victims of this myth. Our society tells women to be demure, quiet and wait to be discovered. At the same time, our society rewards those who get off their duffs, sell their ideas, and make things happen. One survey of fired executives revealed that 83 percent of them had the common trait of not aggressively pointing out their achievements to their superiors. Rather, they waited to have their efforts discovered. As Will Rogers put it, "Even if you're on the right track, you'll get run over if you just sit there."

The antidote to this myth is obvious. Promote thyself. Get out and push your ideas, because if you don't, no one else will. It's okay to tactfully blow your own horn. After all, if you don't, how is anyone else to know your tune?

Myth #6—Ideas Are Like Magic. You Don't Have to Work for Them.

The miraculous-inspiration myth would have you believe that creative ideas are flashes of brilliance that suddenly appear out

*Ted Schwarz, *The Successful Promoter* (Chicago: Contemporary Book, Inc., 1976), p. vii.

of the blue to a fortunate few. One only has to be in the right place at the right time and presto! Instant creativity and success descends on the lucky recipient. The problem with this myth is the same as the previous one—if you believe it, nothing will happen. Flashes of brilliance come to those who work for them. Any successful artist, writer, inventor or creative professional can attest to the absurdity of waiting to be inspired. First you begin and then the insights appear. Magical insights and solutions to problems are sometimes stumbled on, but they are almost without exception stumbled on by people who happen to be studying the problem.

There is a term used to describe the behavior of those who wait to be inspired—*procrastination.*

Myth #7—Creative Thinking Is Nice but Impractical

If you've read this far and believe this myth, go back to the beginning and start over. You haven't been paying attention.

Myth #8—Creativity Means Complexity

Edward R. Murrow once remarked, "The obscure we see eventually. The completely obvious, it seems, takes longer." In an age of specialization, where technology is king, it's easy to fall for the complexity myth. Trips to the moon, nuclear power, solid-state circuitry, integrated computer systems—who can understand it all? Most of us wonder who can understand any of it.

As a result of being mesmerized by technology we usually conclude one of two things: (1) new ideas in today's world are simply over our heads. Therefore don't waste your time trying to understand them or be creative. Or (2) new ideas in today's world aren't over our heads but they have to be complicated to be of value. If it's simpler or obvious, forget it. The first conclusion leads to immobilization and the second leads to needless overcomplication. Simpler, quicker, better and cheaper ideas are often overlooked. Many of us have heard the story of the team of engineers who were called out to solve the problem of dislodging a truck that was stuck in an underpass. True to their profession, they took an engineering approach and began making a series of complex stress calculations. A small boy standing by asked one of the engineers, "Hey, mister, why don't you let the air out of the tires?" The problem was instantly solved.

Best-selling author Robert Ringer summarized how complexity can overshadow or even destroy creativity. He wrote:

> Looking back over my past, I'm amazed at how far out of my way I went to complicate my business dealings. The time and money spent on building large organizations, setting up complex corporate structures and operating coast to coast seem incomprehensible to me now. The result was that I never had time to do the one thing which really makes the big dollars—tap my creative abilities. All my hours were tied up in seeking ways to make things complicated.

The complexity myth is overcome by realizing that all other things being equal, simpler is better. Look for the simple solution or idea first. Einstein put it this way: "Everything should be made as simple as possible. But not simpler."

Myth #9—The Best Way Has Already Been Found

The best-way trap is an outgrowth of our natural craving for certainty. Because people demand certainty, social institutions set themselves up as providers of it. Schools spend years teaching you *the* answers to questions and *the* solutions to problems. Numerous religious sects will gladly tell you *the* way to a utopian afterlife. For years Walter Cronkite told us "That's *the way* it is."

One-way thinking is an archenemy of creativity because it prohibits anything else from being better. The result is a tunnel-vision approach to living where yesterday's solutions are used to solve today's problems. We have only to look back in time to see the absurdity of this type of thinking. Millions of lives have been lost over religious wars where "my way is *the* way" thinking was the major issue. Experts once were sure that the world was flat. Medical science once believed the cure for illnesses was to bleed people. And if you want a more contemporary example, remember that Hitler's attempt to exterminate minorities was termed "the final solution."

The problem in our day-to-day living is that one-way thinking forecloses an open mind. As Abraham Maslow put it, "If the only tool you have is a hammer, you tend to see every problem as a nail."

In his book *The Teaching of Elementary Science and Mathematics*, Alexander Calandra tells of a classic encounter between a creative student and a physics professor. On an examination the student was given the following problem: "Show how it is possible to determine the height of a tall building with the aid of a barometer." Refusing to parrot back the one solution taught in class, the student answered, "Take the barometer to the top of the building, attach a long rope to it, lower the barometer to the street and then bring it up, measuring the length of the rope. The length of the rope is the height of the building."

The student protested not receiving any credit for his answer, and Calandra was called in to act as an arbiter. The professor contested that the student's answer didn't certify competence in the knowledge of physics and Calandra gave the student six minutes to come up with an answer that would demonstrate such proficiency. The student then wrote, "Take the barometer to the top of the building and lean over the edge of the roof. Drop the barometer, timing its fall with a stopwatch. Then, using the formula $S = \frac{1}{2} at^2$, calculate the height of the building." The professor conceded and Calandra gave the student almost full credit. As he left with the student, Calandra asked the young man if he had any other answers to the problem. "Oh yes. There are many ways of getting the height of a tall building with the aid of a barometer." He suggested the following:

- Take the barometer out on a sunny day and measure the length of the barometer and its shadow. Then measure the length of the building's shadow, and by the use of a simple proportion you can determine the height of the building.

- Climb the stairs of the building with the barometer and, as you do this, mark off the length of the barometer along the wall. You then count the number of marks, and this will give you the building's height in barometer units. A simple, direct measure.
- Take the barometer to the basement of the building and knock on the superintendent's door. When he answers, tell him, "Mr. Superintendent, here I have a fine barometer. If you will tell me the height of this building, I will give you this barometer."

The best-way trap is snapped by opening your eyes to the reality that there are no final solutions to anything. Newer and better ways to do anything can always be found. Rigid, inflexible thinking is a great killer of creative ability. As Friedrich Nietzsche put it:

This way is *my* way. . . .
What is your way?
The way doesn't exist.

IDEA TRAPS FURTHER COMPOUND THE PROBLEM

Myths about creativity aren't the only internal pitfalls to innovation. We also have myths about ourselves that stifle creativity. I call them idea traps—common, erroneous self-concepts that keep us from utilizing our creative potential. Once again, these messages are acquired from societal institutions such as parents, teachers, religion, the media, the government and so on. As you read the following eight idea traps, see if you can recall a time or times when one or more of these injunctions kept you from doing something unique or unusual that you wanted to do.

Trap #1 — I'm Too Old

According to T. Harry Thompson, "Age improves wine, compound interest and nothing else I can think of." No offense, T. Harry, but if you really believe that, you haven't been doing much thinking about aging and creativity potential.

The I'm-too-old trap is the favorite cop-out for not trying in our youth-oriented society. Yet history is filled with examples of creative persons whose greatest works came in their later years. George Bernard Shaw won a Nobel Prize when he was nearly seventy. When Thomas Jefferson retired to Monticello, he thought up numerous gadgets and innovations while in his seventies and eighties. Dr. George Washington Carver was still turning out useful ideas for agriculture at eighty. Alexander Graham Bell perfected the telephone at fifty-eight and solved the problem of stabilizing the balance in airplanes while in his seventies. Mark Twain wrote two books, *Eve's Diary* and *The $30,000 Bequest*, at seventy-one. Benjamin Franklin produced one of his greatest works of writing at eighty-four. The list of examples is endless.

There is scholarly evidence that indicates creative ability may well be ageless, if, in fact, not aided by age. Professor Harvey Lehman in a study of approximately one thousand creative achievements listed the median age of the creators at seventy-four when creativity occurred.

All indications are that the more we use our creative abilities, the better they become. In the words of Somerset Maugham, "Imagination grows by exercise and contrary to popular belief is more powerful in the mature than in the young." Ideas for exercising your imagination are discussed in Chapter Three. For now, the key to beating the I'm-too-old trap is this: Don't confuse aging with stagnation. There's one helluva difference.

Trap #2 — I'm Too Busy

"Gee, I'd love to be creative, but who's got the time? I have a spouse, job, children and numerous social activities. How on earth can you expect me to find time to think?" Does that sound like you? For most of us time is *the* scarce resource. Few of us have enough, but everyone has all there is. We talk about the passage of time. Time doesn't pass on, we do.

We've all heard that time is money, but turn the proverb around and you've got a real truism—money is time. Many highly successful people discovered long ago that the key to riches is found in taking the time to sit back, innovate, dream, plan and calculate how to turn their ideas into realities. Most of us are so preoccupied with the business of day-to-day living that we deny ourselves the opportunities of concentrating our time on major projects with large payoffs. We scramble for nickels and dimes when we could be quietly reaching out and picking up dollars.

The time trap is beaten by accepting the fact that the only way you create time for innovation is to steal it from some other present activity. Waiting until you have the time to innovate is as futile as trying to save money by putting away what you don't happen to spend. Ideas to help you make the time for your creative endeavors can be found in Chapter Ten.

Trap #3—What Will Other People Think?

The conformity trap is still another way that we allow our creative abilities to be hindered. Approval seeking is the primary motive of much of our behavior, and many of us have been taught that such behavior is the major justification for our existence. The unwritten social messages come through loud and clear from the time we are old enough to understand:

Look like everyone else—"We like our salesmen to wear white shirts and wing-tipped shoes."
Don't be you—"Why can't you be quiet like your sister?"
Try to please everyone—"If you take your complaint to the boss, Bill's going to be very upset. Better not rock the boat."
Behave like everyone else—"All the other kids like to play baseball. What's wrong with you?"
Think like everybody else—"How can you believe such

nonsense? No one else does. What you need is a brain transplant."

Ironically, those who crave approval the most are usually the last to get it. If you're just like everyone else, who needs you? There are millions more just like you. Moreover, to try to please everyone is to dream the impossible dream. No matter what you do, a certain percentage of people will dislike you a certain percentage of the time. And the more successful you become, the more you can count on the percentages to rise.

Trying to please the group means thinking like the group, and that excludes thinking for yourself. I'm not suggesting that you assume the role of an anticonformist, banana-brained idiot, who advocates the exact opposite of society's wishes. If you do that, you're still letting the group do your thinking for you. Do your own thinking. Trust your own feelings and behave accordingly. Remember, the person who makes money in the stock market buys when everyone else is selling, and vice versa. Joan Brannon said it best: "He who walks in another's tracks leaves no footprints."

As for worrying about what other people might think—forget it. They aren't concerned about you. They're too busy worrying about what you and other people think of them.

Trap #4—I Don't Have the Proper Credentials

You're in the credentials trap if you believe that tomorrow's new ideas will come exclusively from those having the proper academic and professional pedigrees. You don't need a professional license or a doctorate in any discipline in order to innovate. I'm not saying credentials are unimportant. However, a lack of credentials shouldn't stop you from trying to innovate as long as you can do so without hurting others. Do you think Thomas Edison had a degree in physics or that Jesus Christ was an ordained priest or minister? Where would we be today if innovators such as Franklin, Ford, Fulton and others had waited for someone to give them the proper credentials before innovating?

If you're eager to learn about something and willing to work at it, don't let the credentials trap stand in your way. Books, libraries, films, cassette tapes and short courses can start you toward learning the basics on your own. And the sheer experience of learning by doing is one of the greatest of educators.

Trap #5—I Might Fail!

If you try to create something new, your endeavors probably will result in frustration and failure many times. It's simply part of the price you pay for meaningful success. It isn't the act of failure itself but rather a negative reaction to it that makes it an idea trap.

A positive reaction to failure allows you to capitalize on it as a learning experience. Thomas Edison tried a hundred times to perfect one of his inventions, each attempt meeting with frustration. When asked if he was discouraged, Edison scoffed at the idea, pointing out that he was making progress. He now knew one hundred things that didn't work. As Al Bernstein remarked, "Success is often the result of taking a misstep in the right direction."

No doubt we have all read about overnight successes, and they do exist. But the very fact of their rarity is what makes them newsworthy: "If at first you do succeed, try to hide your astonishment." Success and failure are merely arbitrary labels placed on given acts and consequences of behavior. They exist only in the mind.

Rudyard Kipling wrote, "Of all the liars in the world, sometimes the worst are your own fears." Get mentally tough with yourself and refuse to let the failure trap stand between you and what you want to do. Just remember this thought from *Success Unlimited* magazine: "Success is never final and failure never fatal. It's courage that counts."

Trap #6—I Work for an Organization; I Can't Be Creative

Honoré de Balzac once defined bureaucracy as a giant mechanism operated by pygmies. Many of us work for large bureaucratic organizations such as corporations, government agencies, universities, public utilities and hospitals. Memos, meetings, policies, procedures, rules and regulations, however well meant, somehow seem to snowball themselves into a mindless quagmire of bureaucratic red tape. All of which leaves precious little time for reflecting and innovating.

Management theorists believe that creative, conceptual skills are the primary ability needed by the members of top management in an organization. Yet all too often the Peter Principle prevails, and those who reach the top do so by following the mindless rules whose reasons for existing have long since vanished. The creative employee frequently leaves or mentally withdraws from his job because he refuses to tolerate the demands of wasted time and effort that the bureaucracy imposes on him. It's a tragic loss for all concerned. And it doesn't have to be that way.

Many organizations, large and small, place a high premium on creativity. If your present employer doesn't tolerate innovation, you're in business with someone who's eventually going nowhere. Why stay on board a ship that at best refuses to weigh anchor and at worst may be sinking? Life is short. Spend your time with those employers who will allow you time to do better things and do things better. Or why not consider starting your own business?

Most importantly, wherever you work, take the initiative and try to innovate before making any negative assumptions. You may be pleasantly surprised.

Trap #7—I'm a Woman; Men Are the Ingenious Ones

Scan any list of geniuses and the fact is that men will far outnumber women. However, as Aaron Levenstein remarked, "Statistics are like a bikini. What they reveal is suggestive but what they conceal is vital." A closer look behind the numbers reveals the extent to which women have been prevented or discouraged from using their creative abilities rather than any innate lack of creative talent. In fact, studies in creative thinking imply that women are at least equal to men in generating new ideas. For example:

- One study testing 702 women revealed their creative aptitude averages as much as 25 percent higher than that of men.
- Another study of 32 high school seniors revealed that the girls showed a 40 percent superiority over the boys in idea fluency.
- In brainstorming sessions, women consistently average more ideas than men.
- After conducting an exploratory study on "Sex-Role Identification and Creative Thinking," the results showed no significant relationships between the total creativity scores and either of the masculinity femininity scores for males or females.

Although not usually recognized, the traditional role of women calls for a lot of creative thinking. It takes imagination to come up with a new way to get an uncooperative baby to eat. It takes imagination to plan meals so that the family won't tire of eating the same old thing. It takes imagination to tastefully redecorate a house or maintain a comfortable standard of living on an inflation-racked budget. The number of ways in which women who stay in the home are forced to use their creativity each day is endless. Yet these are creative achievements which will never find their way into the record books.

Even when they have demonstrated great creative potential, women have usually been discouraged from pursuing their dreams and encouraged to conform to the traditional domestic role. Although things are getting better, too many talented, intelligent women are relegated to servile positions in industry which call for little or no use of their creative talents. It's an enormous waste of human potential.

Imagineering calls for creative thinking and *action*. As the studies point out, women are excellent creative thinkers. The solution to this trap is to wake up to the powers of your own imagination and assert yourself by following through. If you're a woman, resolve to do more than think. Resolve to act. Take one idea, no matter how small, and carry it out. Resolve to finish what you start, no matter what. The techniques presented in Chapters Eight through Eleven will show you how.

Trap #8—I Don't Have a High I.Q.

If you were educated in the United States in the past thirty years, you probably took many of the so-called intelligence tests designed to measure your intellectual potential. The problem isn't with the people who design these tests but with the people who insist on using them as arbitrary measures of human potential. Those who design these tests make no fantastic claims for their predictability and realize that it is absurd to think you can reduce something as complex as human potential to a number. However, all too often these tests fall into the hands of teachers and administrators who use them as labels for stereotyping the abilities of students. The result is the mental equivalent of turning a chimpanzee loose with a machine gun. There is no faster way to make a low achiever out of an impressionable young person than to label him or her as one. No doubt the labels enhance the self-image of those who do well on these tests. But each winner comes at the cost of labeling many others as losers.

With respect to creativity, intelligence tests aren't designed to measure creative ability. Therefore, to assess your creative potential on the basis of intelligence test scores is even more absurd. As Dr. L. L. Thurstone wrote, "To be extremely intelligent is not the same as to be gifted in creative work. Students with high intelligence are not necessarily the ones who produce the most original ideas. The quiz kids are often referred to as geniuses. They would undoubtedly score high in memory functions. . . . But it is doubtful whether they are also fluent in producing new ideas."

The I.Q. trap is beaten by recognizing it for what it is—an arbitrary label, and nothing more. Allowing labels to define your abilities in any endeavor is just another way that you prevent yourself from doing what you want to do or becoming what you want to become. Pretty ridiculous, isn't it?

LIBERATE YOUR MIND

Bill Vaughn once wrote, "People learn something every day, and a lot of the time it's that what they learned the day before was wrong." What was just presented is a partial list of all the psychological myths and snares that can inhibit your creative potential. One way to defeat irrational thinking is to see it for what it is. Therefore, a prerequisite to profitable imagineering is to liberate your mind by exploding the creativity myths and springing the idea traps that inhibit your creative abilities. Try exercising your own creative abilities by seeing if you can't think of any additional beliefs about creativity that may be holding you back.

Letting go of beliefs that you've held on to for years is never easy. Change is tough but it's a worthwhile investment in your own growth. As Gelett Burgess remarked, "If in the last few years you haven't discarded a major opinion or acquired a new one, check your pulse. You may be dead."

2

Imagineering Begins with Deciding What You Want

"You've removed most of the roadblocks to success when you've learned the difference between motion and direction."

—Bill Copeland

IF NECESSITY IS the mother of invention, then goals must be the father. One of the most amazing things to me is the way that new ideas and opportunities come to those who decide what they want and have the courage to pursue it. It's the closest thing to real magic that I know of.

WHY GOALS ARE SO IMPORTANT

Goal setting is the first of four major steps in the process of imagineering your way to success. If you ask a successful person what they think about goals, you will undoubtedly find goal setting to be one of their most important of activities. Goals are important for several reasons.

They Fill a Basic Need

It's a basic tenet of psychology that behavior is goal-directed. Any act doesn't just happen. It happens for a reason.

To put it another way, human beings are goal-seeking creatures. Goals are necessary for our very health and survival. If you doubt this, check out the rates of illness and mortality when people are stripped of their sense of purpose. Persons who retire without something to retire to have higher incidences of mortality and illness than those who continue working.

In contrast, as I pointed out in Chapter One, many creative people find their final years are frequently the most productive. Why is this? Is it because they are a gifted, higher order of beings? I think not. Rather, it's because they have carved out an ongoing sense of direction and purpose to their lives. They're absorbed in what they are doing and eager to give life all that they have to offer. And as if by magic, life returns the favor by being fuller, richer and longer. All of us, young and old alike, need goals because they give us reasons for being and doing. And this is a basic psychological need.

They Serve as a Vehicle for Channeling Your Time, Effort and Ideas

A well-thought-out system of goals and objectives gives continuity to your endeavors. An old axiom from the Koran says, "If you don't know where you're going, any road will get you there." Goals prevent this problem from occurring, if we keep them in focus.

One of today's greatest roadblocks to meaningful achievement is that most of us get caught up in activities. We become so immersed in activity that we lose sight of what we're doing and the activity becomes a false end in itself rather than a means to an end. The most successful people know how to carry out complex activities while keeping their eye on long-range results. If the goals change, they change. Those in the activity trap continue the same behavior long after the goals have changed.

With respect to creative efforts, consider the goal John F. Kennedy set in 1960 to place a man on the moon by 1970. It kindled the imagination of an entire nation, and millions set about concentrating their time and efforts toward achieving this ultimate goal. Ideas were generated by the tens of millions with the result that a seemingly visionary pipe dream became a reality in ten years.

On an individual level, goals can do the same thing for you. One ingredient of achieving anything major is to invest a portion of today's time, energy and thinking into projects with potentially high, long-range payoffs. Without a sound system of goals this is nearly impossible.

Goals Provide a Foundation for Personal Growth and Self-Esteem

This is one of the major by-products of goals: confidence building. As you begin to set goals and meet them, you feel the personal pride and enjoy the benefits of their achievement. As a result, you set bigger goals, dream bigger dreams and reach them. You develop a sense of self-reliance and self-trust that is ever so necessary for large successes. And with belief in self comes peace of mind, which in turn increases your capacity to excel. This whole process is best illustrated by what I call the success cycle.

2. Goal Achievement

1. Goal Setting

3. Satisfaction and Pride

4. Increased Self-Confidence

Goals Make Life Interesting and Exciting

Do you know someone who is bored with life or lacks enthusiasm and zeal? Ask them what their goals are and you'll probably find them to be vague, meager, or nonexistent.

Most of us make the mistake of thinking that a zest for living is beyond our control. Nothing could be further from the truth. As Neil Sedaka sings, "You gotta make your own sunshine," and one good way to do that is to set meaningful goals and begin pursuing them *immediately*.

Too few of us seem to realize that immobilization isn't the result of depression. It's the cause. It is difficult, if not impossible, to be absorbed in pursuing a meaningful goal and be depressed at the same time. Just as there is a success cycle, there is a failure cycle which looks like this:

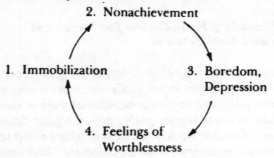

2. Nonachievement

1. Immobilization

3. Boredom, Depression

4. Feelings of Worthlessness

The failure cycle is all based on one simple assumption: "There's really nothing I can do." And from nothing, nothing comes. On the other hand, the success cycle is based on the assumption "There's always something I can do," and as a result these people feel free, in charge and enthusiastic about their lives.

Goals Are the Backbone of a Positive Attitude

Have you ever known anyone who created anything meaningful with attitudes that were ultimately negative? I haven't. A positive outlook is the one common denominator of every successful imagineer I've ever had the pleasure of knowing.

It's true that some people credit their success to what can be described as positive pessimism. Every time they approach an endeavor, they expect to fail. However, they also realize that if they keep learning and trying they will ultimately succeed. They use positive pessimism as a buffer to prevent frustrations from disillusioning them and causing them to give up. However, their basic premise is one of ultimate success. In effect they say to themselves, "I can't win them all but I can't lose them all either."

A positive mental attitude is a necessary asset when it comes to creative achievement. And the very foundation of a positive outlook is contained in goal setting. When you set goals for yourself, you make a commitment to optimism by deciding to take steps that will ensure a better future for you and yours. And this increased expectation of a brighter future coupled with the satisfaction of seeing your ideas become realities makes for very enjoyable present moments too.

IF PERSONAL GOAL SETTING IS SO GREAT, WHY IS IT SO RARE?

Admittedly, few of us make the effort and take the time to sit back and give serious thought to what we want out of life. Yet time after time all of us have seen how the future belongs to those who decide what they want and have the drive to go after it. When I ask people why they don't set goals for themselves, I get some interesting and generally irrational answers. Here are six of the most common excuses that people give. Do any of these sound like you?

"Making such big decisions is just too hard"

The hidden message behind this excuse is "It's easier to forget about the future and let tomorrow take care of itself. I'll take the easy way out and just hope for the best." This approach to living has all the rationality of an ostrich burying its head in the sand. No doubt, becoming overly concerned with the future can keep us from enjoying the present. However, to totally ignore the future makes you a slave to it rather than the master of it. Decisions about your future are an opportunity to control your future, and taking the easy way out has a hidden price tag that too many of us have found to be exorbitant.

"It's too risky"

Like the first excuse, this one also has a hidden message, which is "What if I don't reach my goals? I won't be able to live with myself." The person who says this to himself has fallen into the common trap of confusing his personal worth with his achievements. It's very easy to do this, considering the fact that this is what society teaches us to do. However, the simple fact is that what you do and what you are are two separate and distinct entities. Your worthiness as a human being is confirmed by the mere fact that you're alive, and no amount of success or failure will change your self-image unless you allow it to.

The greatest risk of all is to not take risks, for it carries with it the overwhelming odds of a wasted life. Everything you want in life involves taking risks. You can't improve your life or anything else in the world without risking. And as for security, Helen Keller said it best:

Security is mostly a superstition. It does not exist in nature, nor do the children of men as a whole experience it. Avoiding danger in the long run is no safer than outright exposure. Life is either a daring adventure or nothing.

"I know my goal: I want to be happy"

If you search for happiness as an end in itself, I promise you this: You won't find it. In today's world most of us don't want happiness. We demand it! In fact, the demand for happiness is so rampant that analysts, authors and seminar leaders are profiting handsomely. Yet the happiest people are those who realize that happiness is a by-product of effective living and not a goal to be achieved at a given time.

Instead of making happiness your goal, view your entire life as an experience to enjoy and be happy about every day. The potential to be happy is greater today than it has ever been in the history of man. Enjoy, and then go about the business of setting yourself some specific and meaningful goals.

"Goals will restrict my freedom and spontaneity"

There is no doubt that achieving major goals requires self-discipline in large quantities. However, it does not logically follow that imposing order on yourself means restricting your personal freedom. The key here is to set your own goals. If you're pursuing a goal that you set for yourself, how can you be restricting your freedom? You're taking the necessary steps to get what you want out of life. Isn't that what freedom is all about?

"Other people always ruin my plans"

The translation of this excuse is classic: "I hereby abdicate all personal responsibility for my future. Other people are in control of my life. This gives me the flexibility to step forward and claim any successes as my own, and blame all my future shortcomings on others." Sound familiar?

It's a natural human failing to look outside ourselves for all the reasons that we can't do something. However, blaming others only leads to frustration on the part of all concerned. If other people control your life, it's simply because you allow them to. Ultimately everyone is responsible for his own feelings, triumphs, satisfactions and misfortunes. To accept this one fact is to take a giant step toward a better life. Albert Ellis summed it up nicely when he wrote:

> The best years of your life are the ones in which you decide your problems are your own. You don't blame them on your mother, the ecology or the President. You realize that you control your own destiny.

"I don't know how to begin"

The rest of this chapter presents a system of guidelines and exercises for setting goals. Once you get into goal setting, you will find it far more enjoyable than you imagined.

TWO EASY WAYS TO MAKE TOUGH DECISIONS

The sheer weight of making decisions about what to do with our lives is what prevents many of us from getting started in

goal setting. Two very helpful tools for overcoming this inertia are the self-discovery test and the categorizing of goals.

Self-Discovery Is the Key to
Understanding Your Wants

It makes little sense to decide what you want out of life until
you have a good idea of who you are. This is why the following self-discovery exercise precedes goal setting. Once you
have established a sense of identity, you will be in a much
better position to set meaningful goals.

Choose a time and place where you can be undisturbed
while performing this exercise. Take ten index cards or slips
of paper and on each card answer the question "Who Am I?"
in a different way. Work rapidly, as the objective of this exercise is to discover your true feelings about yourself. Don't
censor any answers that come into your mind. Answers such
as gambler or ping-pong fiend are no less valid than answers
like human being, parent, student, wife, homeowner, or sports
fan.

If you find you need more than ten cards, fine. Use as
many as you need. If you have trouble coming up with ten
answers, relax and stop judging your answers. There are no
right or wrong answers to this exercise. The key is to be spontaneous and capture your initial thoughts.

When you are finished listing all the "I ams," read them,
rank them in order of importance and number them. Then turn
over the first card and complete the following statement: "This
'I am' is first because——." Do the same for the remaining
cards in order.

When you finish ranking the cards, take time to look them
over and reflect on them. Imagine these cards were written by
someone else and write answers to the followng questions:

1. What do these cards tell you about this person?
2. What things are most important to him/her?
3. What types of things would this person enjoy doing with
his/her life that you aren't doing?

4. If this person had only six months to live, how would you recommend he/she spend them?

Be sure to keep the self-discovery cards and answers to the above questions. You will want to refer to them as you formulate your goals.

Break Down Your Goals into Manageable Categories

This exercise is the first step toward specifying the goals that you ultimately will be pursuing. Take six or more index cards or sheets of paper and label each one with the following headings: career goals, personal-relationship goals, recreational goals, personal-growth goals, material goals and prestige goals. Next pick up each card and write down some goals that you would like to achieve in each of these areas. As in the first exercise, work rapidly and don't censor your impulses. If you think you would like to do it, it's a potential goal. Go for quantity. It's okay to list a goal in several categories.

When you complete this exercise, go back and mark the two most important goals in each category. This narrows your field of goals to a total of twelve. Record them on another sheet of paper and from this list choose the three most important ones. This now gives you three very important goals that you can go about refining, specifying and thinking about how you can achieve. And three important goals are plenty. Finally, rank these three in order of importance.

GUIDELINES FOR FORMALIZING GOALS

You now should have a rough idea about three important things you would like to accomplish. The task now is to refine, shape and polish these ideas into some formal goals for you to pursue. The following guidelines if consciously followed will ultimately spell the difference between successes and pipe dreams.

Be Sure Your Goals Are Your Goals

If you're the one who plans to innovate and imagineer, you will be much more committed to carrying out those things that you want to do. Don't let anyone set your important goals for you. It's your life. Take charge and do those things that are most meaningful to you. Realize also that there are a myriad of forces such as parents, employers, the government and whatever that would rather you pursue their goals and not your own. Stand firm on this point. The only true success in life is in living it your own way.

This doesn't mean being an obstinate individual or not soliciting advice on what your goals should be. Friends, relatives and employers can all be helpful in providing you with ideas for goals that you may not have thought up on your own. However, reserve the right to make the final decision on your own goals. If a goal is set by you and is something you really want to achieve, the chances for success are immensely improved.

Put Them in Writing

Writing down your goals is important for two reasons. First, it helps you clearly identify what you want. Most of us just think about goals and never write them down. However, all too often undocumented thoughts vanish into thin air, and if that thought is an important goal, it runs the high risk of never being realized. Written goals are far less likely to be forgotten or lost in the shuffle of daily activity.

The second reason for writing goals is that it increases your personal commitment to them. You're investing more of yourself in the goal and this is one investment whose potential payoff is very high. If it's an important goal, be sure to write it down.

Make Your Goals Challenging but Attainable

Good goals cause you to stretch and grow in order to achieve them. If you set a goal that is easily attainable, it won't give you much satisfaction and you will likely lose interest in achieving it. At the other extreme, setting what you perceive as an impossible goal will also result in little or no motivation. It's hard to get yourself up to fight a losing battle, unless you happen to be a masochist. Search out those goals that will require meaningful attention but that you feel you can achieve. What is an attainable goal is a very personal decision, but if you think you can, you can. Go after it.

Goals Should Be as Specific and Measurable as Possible

The more specific a goal is, the more direction it will give you. For example, don't say, "I want to be financially independent." Instead say, "I want to accumulate net assets of one million dollars by age sixty." Don't say, "I want a better job." What kind of job? Making how much money? In what industry? Requiring what skills? Working in what type of environment? By when? Sit down with a pencil and paper and try to specify as clearly as you can what it is that you want. This can save you an enormous amount of time and effort.

Admittedly, not all goals are easy to measure. Goals such as being a good citizen or a responsible employee are more difficult to quantify. In these cases you can construct a rating scale from one to ten, with one representing the poorest performance and ten representing the best. Then you can estimate where on the scale you think you are now and decide where you would like to be.

If the rating-scale approach doesn't work, try verbally describing what you want as clearly as you can. For example, if you want to dress up your home, answer questions such as How can I improve the floors, the windows, the ceilings, the bedrooms, the den, the lawn and so on. Answers to these questions will give you much more direction than simply saying, "I want a better-looking home."

Finally, if you find that you cannot quantify it, measure it, rate it, or describe it, you probably can forget it as a goal.

Major Goals Must Be Compatible

It's easy to fall into the trap of setting important goals where the attainment of one prevents the achievement of the other. For example, you want to take an ocean cruise on your vacation, but this means you won't be able to afford the down payment on your dream home this year. You want to excel in both tennis and golf, but you don't have enough leisure time to practice them both. These are examples of incompatible goals.

Worse yet, incompatible goals can lead you into putting your efforts into several projects and achieving no major goals at all. After you decide on your major goals, check them for compatibility. It can prevent a lot of frustration and wasted effort.

Goals Should Be Subject to Revision and Change

Just because you set a meaningful goal today doesn't necessarily mean it will have meaning for you tomorrow. At the age of six you may have wanted to be a fireman, at twenty a doctor and at forty a painter. As a growing human being you have to expect that changes and preferences for what you want to do will be forever changing and evolving. Consequently, don't think of your goals as something carved in stone for the ages. In fact, it's a good idea to periodically update and revise your major goals.

Thinking of your goals as rigid and inflexible may keep you from setting them or from having goals that contribute to your own satisfaction and fulfillment. A good system of goals provides direction but it's also capable of accommodating growth and change.

Every Goal Should Have a Target Date

Never think of a goal as a goal until you set a deadline for accomplishment. Goals without deadlines are daydreams. In conjunction with this, whenever you set a major goal be sure to break it down into subgoals and list the activities necessary to achieve the subgoals. Subgoals should also have deadlines that should be realistic and allow time for errors, mishaps and the unforeseen.

When setting target dates it helps to consider goals from a relative time perspective. For purposes of simplicity let's discuss goals in terms of:

Long-range goals—Results you want to accomplish or experience in your lifetime. Usually these goals will take more than one year to achieve.

Intermediate goals—Goals you want to accomplish in less than one year.

Daily goals—Seeing that you make the most of each day. (Daily goals are discussed in Chapter Ten.) All these goals must be considered in light of each other. What you want is a system of goals where your shorter-range goals contribute to your long-range ones. This concept of co-ordinating a hierarchy of goals is called *goal congruency*. Such a practice helps you to make the best use of your time and energy and prevents you from spinning your wheels. Meaningful achievement comes from being able to make today's small effort count toward a lifetime of great results.

Putting deadlines on your goals and subgoals is a major key to increasing your motivation and commitment to achieving them. Set target dates that challenge you but don't make you feel overly hurried or pressured. Achieving subgoals creates the satisfaction and momentum that will spur you on toward achieving your major goal.

Establish Criteria for Success at the Beginning

Success is a very personal thing. Therefore, criteria for success should be set by you and only you. However, it's an excellent idea to establish criteria at the outset. Like deadlines, success measurements can create enthusiasm and give you benchmarks of progress along the way.

When establishing success criteria, don't fall into the trap of thinking in simplistic success-failure terms. Think in terms of degrees of success. Set optimistic, realistic and pessimistic criteria for success. For example, if you're a marketing executive planning strategy for a new product, your optimistic, realistic and pessimistic criteria for success might be $100,000, $80,000 and $60,000 of sales. This means the best you can hope for is $100,000 sales volume, and if misfortune strikes, $60,000 is the lowest acceptable volume. However, you expect sales to hover around the $80,000 level for the coming year. Establishing a range of success criteria enables you to better evaluate the results of your efforts than if you simply set one goal and consider anything less than that a failure. Give yourself a range, rather than an arbitrary figure, and most importantly, don't confuse your degree of success with your self-worth.

Set Priorities for Your Goals

The reason that most major goals aren't achieved is simply because we spend our time doing second things first. Every set of goals should be ranked in order of importance. And the majority of your efforts put into achieving the most important goals.

How finely you go about distinguishing priorities is a matter of personal choice. You could simply concentrate on the two or three most important goals chosen in the goal-setting exercise. Or you could divide each set of short-, medium-, and long-range goals into three categories:

A. Must do
B. Should do
C. Nice to do

Then, number the goals in each category according to its importance. Your most important goal is labeled A1, second most important A2, and so on. For example, let's assume it's New Year's Eve. A list of intermediate goals and priorities for the coming year might look as follows:

Priority	Goal
A1	Spend two hours each day with my children.
B2	Take spouse to New York.
C4	Volunteer for charity work.
C2	Learn scuba diving.
C3	Take speed-reading course.
B3	Expand product line.
A2	Increase sales by 20 percent.
C1	Enclose carport.
C5	Plant vegetable garden.
B4	Take family to Disneyland.
C6	Lower golf score by ten strokes.
B1	Lose fifteen pounds.

Whatever priority system you use, just be sure to do it. Some people simply number their list while others label their goals Ace, King, Queen and Jack. Choose a style that works for you and stick to it.

Pareto's Law or the 80/20 Rule explains why setting priorities is so important. Named after Vilfredo Pareto, a nineteenth-century Italian economist, this rule states that in a large number of items, 80 percent of the value of the items can be found in 20 percent or less of the items. There are plenty of examples in life that tend to validate the 80/20 Rule. For example, 80 percent of the dollar value of an inventory can be found in 20 percent of the items. Eighty percent of all television viewing is spent watching 20 percent of all programs. Eighty percent of the dirt on floors in an office is concentrated in 20 percent of the office space (the aisles). Eighty percent of your telephone calls come from 20 percent or less of your callers.

The 80/20 Rule applies to goals also. Eighty percent of your achievement can be found by meeting 20 percent or less of your goals. The key is that they must be your most important goals. Setting priorities is a must.

AN ACTION-PLANNING EXERCISE

Intermediate goals or projects bridge the gap between daily activities and lifetime achievements. They give us a dimension of direction and usually take less than one year but more than one day to achieve. They're an essential ingredient in creating a productive and useful life. For example, my intermediate goal at this moment is to complete this book.

The following is an exercise in thinking through an intermediate-range goal that you would like to achieve. Take several sheets of paper and answer the following questions and statements:

1. State clearly and specifically a goal you would like to achieve in the next six months.
2. Why do you want to achieve this goal?
3. If you succeed, what will it do for you?
4. What will you consider to be a moderate success? A good success? A tremendous success? Be specific.
5. How much do you want to achieve this goal?
6. How will achieving this goal contribute to the attainment of longer-range goals?
7. What price will you have to pay to achieve this goal: Are you willing to pay it?
8. Estimate your chances of achieving this goal.

9. What will happen if you aren't successful?

10. List the major subgoals involved in achieving this goal and assign a target date to each.

11. What obstacles stand between you and successful completion of this project? How will you overcome them?

12. What can you do today that will start you on the path to achieving this goal?

Put Up Signs to Remind You of Your Most Important Goals

This is one good way to keep yourself from falling into the activity trap. If you're constantly reminded of what your major goal is, the odds of losing sight of it in a whirlwind of activity are reduced, if not eliminated.

By putting up signs, I'm not suggesting billboards to advertise your goals to the world. Perhaps you can simply write the goal on a card and tape it to your desk or the dashboard of your car. Or you might put it in your wallet or some place that you will frequently have to see it. If your goal is to lose weight, tape a card with your ideal weight on your refrigerator door. The main idea is to place the reminder where you will see it frequently and where it will be most effective.

According to an anonymous philosopher, "When you're up to your waist in alligators, it's difficult to remind yourself that your initial objective was to drain the swamp." Well-placed reminders can be very effective in snatching you from the jaws of the activity trap.

Visualizing Achieving Your Goals

Harry Emerson Fosdick wrote, "Hold a picture of yourself long and steadily enough in your mind's eye and you will be drawn toward it...Great living starts with a picture held in your imagination of what you would like to do or be." Go back and reread that quote several times. It contains an enormous amount of wisdom and a key secret to any type of success. The successful sales person pictures the customer buying as he makes his presentation. The successful athlete imagines the joy of victory as he practices. The successful author pictures his book in a bookstore window as he writes and rewrites. The successful student pictures himself as a doctor, lawyer, engineer, executive, or whatever he aspires to be as he puts in endless hours studying. The list of examples is endless.

Try this exercise. Each day set aside ten minutes or more and visualize the achievement of your most important goal. Close your eyes and block yourself from interruptions and distractions. Imagine the achieving of your goals in as great a detail as possible. If, for example, your goal is to build a new home, visualize the entire house in detail. What does it look like? Where is it located? How is the yard landscaped? Picture each individual room. How is it furnished? What do the drapes look like? What color is each room painted? How does it feel to be living there? How's the view from the living room?

Obviously there is much more to achieving a goal than imagining success. However, you have to think success before you can experience it and visualization is a powerful tool to that end. The seeds of great achievement are almost always sown in great vision.

Have Goals beyond Your Goals

Most of us have a natural tendency to let up as we approach the achievement of a major goal. One way to prevent this from happening is to have another goal ready to pursue after you achieve and enjoy the rewards of the one you are working on.

I'm not advocating a treadmill approach to goal setting where you never let up. Indeed, that's one way to burn yourself out. However, we all need goals to maintain our interest and enjoyment in life. None of us should ever run out of things to do and new horizons to conquer. As George Bernard Shaw remarked, "A perpetual holiday is a good working definition of hell."

Although it may not seem terribly creative, goal setting is a basic step in the imagineering process. Until you know what you want, it makes little sense to generate new solutions to problems and new ideas to transform into successful realities. With a well-charted course, you can begin exercising your imagination and generating productively creative ideas. The next four chapters will show you how.

PART II

GENERATING
AND
PROCESSING IDEAS

3

Understanding and Igniting Your Creative Abilities

"Bring in ideas and entertain them royally, for one of them may be king."

—Mark Van Doren

A DOCTOR ONCE remembered how he signaled to childhood friends by tapping on a hollow log. From this thought, he conceived and eventually invented the stethoscope.

Clarence Birdseye took a trip to Canada and ate some fish that had been naturally frozen and thawed. He borrowed the idea from nature, and the frozen-food industry was born.

Somewhere along the line, an ingenious soul realized that wherever there are pens there must be ink. Why not combine the two: The result was the invention of the fountain pen.

The heart of all new ideas lies in the borrowing, adding, combining or modifying of old ones. Do it by accident and people call you lucky. Do it by design and they'll call you creative. There is a lot of truth to the old axiom that nothing is new under the sun. However, all these old things can be combined in infinitely many ways. And that is the essence of how to be creative.

Understanding that the cornerstone of new ideas lies in the association of old ones gives all of us the ability to create ideas almost at will. The problem is to understand and utilize the processes, techniques and environment that allow us to do it most efficiently and effectively.

Think of your creative abilities as a mental muscle. In order to get the most from this muscle, you need to know:

1. How it works
2. Under what conditions it works best
3. How to exercise it in order to strengthen it and increase its capacity to work for you
4. How to use it

51

UNDERSTANDING THE CREATIVE PROCESS

It's generally agreed by students and practitioners of creativity that the act of developing new ideas goes through a somewhat predictable cycle that will occur over varying periods of time. For purposes of simplicity this process can be divided into five steps.

First Insight

The very seeds of creation are sown in this first phase of the creative cycle. You realize that you have a problem you want to solve or an activity you want to do, and this is the first moment that it occurs to you. You want a better job. You need a darkroom. You have an idea for a story you want to develop or a landscape you want to paint. The company you own produces a waste material that you want to turn into a profitable by-product. All of these are examples of first insight. Realize that this step may occur months or even years before the actual generation of ideas. However, it is the first and a necessary step in the process.

Preparation

With a germinal idea conceived, the next step is to investigate thoroughly all the possibilities and ways in which this idea can be developed and expanded. The creator utilizes all his senses and takes in as much information as he can about the subject. He reads, takes notes, talks to others, asks questions, collects information and explores as much as he can. Arthur Hailey lived as a paying guest at the Roosevelt Hotel in New Orleans while gathering research for his novel *Hotel*. To prepare for writing *Moby Dick*, Herman Melville read every account of whaling he could get his hands on. With respect to painters, Picasso remarked, "The artist is a receptacle for emotions that come from all over the place; from the sky, from the earth, from a scrap of paper, from a passing shape, from a spider's web. . . . A painter paints to unload himself of feelings and visions."

The paradox of creativity is that in order to think up new ideas we must first familiarize ourselves with the ideas of others. And these ideas form a springboard for launching our own imaginations.

Incubation

Once you have immersed yourself with information, the next step is to let your right brain take over. Don't work on the problem. Forget about it. This period of incubation is where you allow your thoughts to go underground and put your subconscious to work.

The incubation period may be long or short, but one thing is certain. It has to occur. Take a walk. Take a nap. Take a bath. Work on another project or a hobby. Forget it for a weekend. Sleep on it. Author Edna Ferber once remarked, "A story must simmer in it's own juice for months or even years before it's ready to serve." Most important insights and decisions are made at the subconscious level. Whether it takes six months, six minutes or six hours, the next stage of the creative process cannot occur until the subconscious mind can do its work.

Illumination

The climax of the creative process occurs at the moment of illumination. Eureka! Suddenly everything falls into place when a sudden, new insight pops into the mind. After long years of study, one day in 1685 Isaac Newton, seeing an apple fall, produced his law of gravitation.

In a similar manner, Charles Darwin gathered information for his theory of evolution. The theory kept eluding him until one day when suddenly it all came together. Darwin wrote, "I can remember the very spot in the road, whilst in my carriage, when to my joy the solution occurred to me."

The seemingly inspirational insights usually happen at the least expected of times. Additionally, there is a large amount of intuition attached to them. Often the creative person is certain that the insight is correct long before he has time to logically confirm it. In his book *The Role of Hunches*, Walter Cannon investigated the creative habits of 232 chemists. The results revealed that over a third of them gave credit to hunches when it came to creative insight. Illumination is also the most exciting and joyous phase of the creative process.

Verification

For all its wondrous insights, illumination can be terribly unreliable. This final phase of the creative process refines the raw material of creative achievement. Intellect and judgment are now brought into play and the hunches and inspirations are logically confirmed or denied. As Henry Eyring put it, "Creativity is rarely a single flash of intuition; it usually requires sustained analysis to separate out the significant factors from the adventitious." You back off and look at your ideas as objectively as possible. You solicit the opinion of others. You revise your good ideas to make them better and often come up with new and improved insights in the process. Ideas generated by illumination need to be tested and refined exhaustively. Both Newton and Darwin spent years elaborating, refining and verifying their theories that appeared at the magic moment of illumination.

Summing up, the key to understanding the creative cycle is to realize that there are five distinct phases, although these phases will not seem logically separated in reality. First there is the initial insight or desire to create, followed by a lengthy period of investigating and information gathering. The third phase is the period of incubation where the subconscious takes over and this gives rise to the moment of illumination when the results of the subconscious efforts come to the surface. Finally, there is a period of refining and verifying the ideas created.

The creative cycle also illustrates the pressing need to develop both sides of our brain in order for us to make the most of our creative powers. First insight, incubation, and illumination are functions of the right brain, while preparation and verification are clearly functions of the left brain. The very heart of creativity lies in a synergistic relationship between the left and right sides of the brain.

CREATE YOURSELF A CREATIVE CLIMATE

Certain conditions and attitudes tend to result in new and better ideas. Thus, in addition to understanding how your creative abilities work, you can further enhance your idea productivity by placing yourself in the proper frame of mind. The following are some of the more common attributes of a creative climate.

Give Yourself an Incentive

You simply, above all, must give yourself a compelling reason for generating new ideas. What's in it for you? Money? Status? A new and better career? A promotion? Self-satisfaction? Just be sure that there's plenty in it for you and you alone. Write down the rewards that you feel you will reap from making the effort to generate new ideas. Human nature dictates that you must do this. The best ideas come from those hungry for success.

Thomas Edison motivated himself through an insatiable urge to make money. Even after becoming wealthy, he once remarked, "Anything that won't sell, I don't want to invent."

Whatever your motives, be sure to establish yourself some personal reward for success. The goal-setting exercises of Chapter Two can be helpful in establishing an incentive.

Put Pressure on Yourself

In addition to giving yourself an incentive, you must create a sense of urgency about coming up with ideas. There is a natural tendency to procrastinate in all of us, and without some degree of pressure, ideas will not develop in worthwhile quantities. Unfortunately, we seem to be our most creative when it comes to thinking up reasons why we can't do something.

Parkinson's Law (work expands to fill the time available) is tremendously applicable to the task of generating new ideas. Give yourself a week to come up with a new idea and you'll take a week to think of one. Give yourself a day and you'll likely come up with one in a day.

You create the necessary pressure by giving yourself reasonable but challenging deadlines for coming up with new ideas *and sticking to them*.

Think Visually

Inasmuch as we live in a left-brain oriented society, most of us do most of our thinking in words and numbers. However, it appears that creative people frequently develop the knack of visualizing and manipulating images in the area in which they are creative. A common technique of creative people is to block out all verbal thoughts and concentrate on forming mental pictures of the subject or problem. For example, Frederich von Kekule's discovery that benzine and other organic molecules are closed chains or rings was the result of a dream in which he saw snakes swallowing their tails. And when describing his creative thought processes, Einstein noted:

> The words or the language as they are written or spoken do not seem to play any role in my mechanism of thought. The psychical entities which seem to serve as elements in thought are certain signs and more or less clear images which can be "voluntarily" reproduced and combined.

Whenever you're trying to generate new ideas, make it a point to concentrate on forming visual images in your mind. Close your eyes and picture the subject or problem you wish to think about in your mind's eye. Block out all verbal thoughts. This can be done by repeating a simple word over and over in your mind until it becomes meaningless. Visual and sensory thinking (right-brain thinking) is much more fluid than verbal thinking, and many new ideas can be induced this way. The resulting visual ideas can be verbally expressed, drawn, or written down later. Thinking in terms of images greatly increases the odds of illumination.

Be Receptive to Your New Ideas

Almost every new innovation you can name came about because some determined idea person stubbornly believed in the products of his or her own imagination. You simply must develop a bullheaded willingness to accept your ideas as useful, worthwhile and valid unless they are totally and conclusively proved wrong.

Related to this is the imperative need to withhold judgment when generating new ideas. To use your judgment and imagination simultaneously is like stepping on the brakes and the accelerator of your car at the same time. Ideas are produced in greatest quantities when judgment is withheld. Only apply judgment after you have generated as many ideas as you can think of.

Creativity is fostered best in a climate of complete receptivity. When you're tempted to be judgmental and creative at the same time, just recognize the statement "That won't work" for what it is—a collection of four-letter words.

Innovate with a Spirit of Playfulness

Creative people usually are known for a spirit of intellectual playfulness and a marked sense of humor. Such traits allow them to approach their work in a relaxed manner, which in turn stimulates their creative abilities.

All of us can enhance our idea-producing capabilities by adopting the same attitudes. Hang loose. Toy at the ideas. Avoid being too careful. Let your mind wonder. Enjoy. Think of creativity as fun even though the results of the fun may be very serious. Such an approach stimulates ideation.

Focus on One Thing at a Time

Creative thinking calls for an atmosphere of relaxed attention that allows us to concentrate our efforts on the subject at hand.

One sure way to jam your creative machinery is to clutter your mind by trying to do several things at once. To try and focus your mental abilities on more than one thing at a time is to attempt the impossible. Face up to the simple fact that you can only do one thing at a time well.

If you try to compose a report and watch television at the same time, or dictate letters and think about the new advertising campaign simultaneously, you will likely find yourself uptight, anxious and overwhelmed by all the tasks before you. Relax, and concentrate on what you're doing now. This will enable you to think most clearly and creatively.

Personal Touches

A final way to set the stage for creative effort is to perform an activity or set a condition which subsequently brings forth your ideas. For example, a friend of mine who is a writer runs several miles before writing. He claims he gets many of his best insights while running.

Writers and thinkers have often come up with some quite strange personal touches to get their creative wheels turning. Friedrich Schiller filled his desk with rotten apples. Marcel Proust had his workroom lined with cork. Mozart exercised, and Samuel Johnson surrounded himself with a purring cat, orange peel and tea. Hart Crane played loud jazz on his Victrola. Immanuel Kant worked in bed with blankets surrounding him in a peculiar formation. All these gimmicks and gadgets aided the particular individual by enhancing his ability to concentrate intensely.

Obviously, I can't tell you what will work for you. Perhaps it's pacing the floor, or a cup of coffee. Or a background noise such as music, television or the steady whirring of a fan may help. There are devices available that generate "white noise" to block out disturbing interruptions and better enable people to concentrate, meditate or sleep. The point is to be alert for these personal touches and use those that work for you.

DEVELOP YOUR IMAGINATION BY EXERCISING IT

Any primary ability or talent can be developed by training. Practice memorizing names or mastering a new language and your memory will improve. Take a course in speed reading and you'll likely double your reading speed and comprehension. Practice doing arithmetic in your head and you'll improve your ability to calculate without a pencil and paper or a calculator.

You can improve your creative ability by exercising it. However, these exercises will benefit you only if you truly *want* to improve your creative capacity. Given an ample amount of desire, the following techniques when properly applied will increase your ability to think up new ideas.

Experience

The best creative exercises provide you with mental activity and material out of which you can form ideas. No other exercise fits this criteria as well as experience. Experience can be firsthand or secondhand, such as reading, listening or spectating. Firsthand experience is far superior. As a Chinese proverb states:

> I hear: I forget
> I see: I remember
> I do: I understand

Highly creative persons usually have a history of a great deal of firsthand experiences in their youth. At age twelve, Edison was employed by the Grand Trunk railroad and he published a newspaper before his fourteenth birthday. While in his teens Edison also bought and sold vegetables and worked in a telegraph office. No doubt his firsthand experience in the work world gave him an early understanding of what types of innovations were needed. By the time he was twenty-two, he perfected and sold the Universal Stock Ticker and sold it to Western Union for $40,000.

All creative exercise involves one type of experience or another. But firsthand experience is the best. A special type of firsthand experience is:

Travel

S. I. Hayakawa remarked, "If you see in any given situation only what everybody else can see, you can be said to be so much of a representative of your culture that you are a victim of it." There's no better way to broaden and refresh your outlook than travel. It gets you out of an environmental rut and exposes you to new people, customs, ideas and ways of living. One key to creative thinking is to view life from a fresh perspective, and travel can give you this new outlook—if you will allow it to. The key to using travel as a creative exercise is to travel actively. Don't simply sign up for a package tour and let the tour guide whisk you from one place to another. Get off the beaten paths and go to the out-of-the-way places. Take time to talk to the people where you visit. Learn what's on their mind. Do they have any unusual customs or ways of doing things? Every culture provides a unique way of looking at common situations and solving common problems. Learning their viewpoint can often provide you with the necessary perspective for generating original ideas.

Carry a camera with you and take lots of shots. Keep a diary or log as you travel. Write down what you experienced and what your impressions were. Later on you can go through your diary and photographs and reflect on your travels. The result is often a new idea. I know a department store window designer who uses travel to provide him with better ideas for his business. Whenever he visits another city or country he photographs store windows, takes notes and, if possible, speaks to other window designers. After returning home he reflects on the information he has gathered and often comes up with a new idea for a window he is working on.

Similarly, you can use travel to develop the imagination of children. For example, one woman was getting ready to take a lengthy train ride with her two children and wanted to keep them occupied for the long journey. Before the trip she told them, "Write down everything you can think up to do on a train ride. I will give you a dime for each good idea you list." The two children came up with 35 good ideas between them.

Self-Reliance

The more you depend on your own ability to think, the more proficient you will become at thinking up new ideas. Experts and consultants should be viewed as collaborators, not dictators. They can provide information for solving problems that would take you much longer to solve alone. No point in reinventing the wheel. However, if you always rely on someone else to solve your problems and tell you what to do, your creative abilities will shrivel rather than flourish for lack of exercise. Try designing a floor plan for your dream home *and then* call in the architect. Formulate your own ideas for a sound retirement plan *and then* call in the financial consultant. Make a list of what you feel are the probable causes of your headaches *and then* see a doctor. In addition to improving your creative abilities, you may save money by discovering that you won't always need the experts—or by making their job easier and faster.

Personal Contacts

One way to learn how to think creatively is to associate yourself with creative people. H. A. Overstreet wrote, "People who are creatively alert are much more interesting than people who are not. They seem to belong to a different species, or perhaps to a higher level of evolution. They see not only what is but what might be; and the power to see what might be is one of the chief traits that distinguish human beings from one another." I'm not suggesting that you must keep company with composers, writers, artists and so on, although these are certainly creative people. Look for people who are fun to talk to and have a keen sense of interest in life. An individual who can stimulate your thought process is what you're looking for. He or she may be a teacher, housewife, plumber or whatever. Essentially, what you're looking for is someone who is not boring. The more you associate with such people, the more

they will force you to exercise your imagination as you interact with them.

One special group of easily accessible and highly creative
people are:

Children

It's been said that insanity is hereditary; you can get it from
your children. Another thing you can get from your children
(or anyone else's) is a great deal of creative exercise.

Preschool-age children are the best candidates because they
haven't had their imaginations impaired by the educational
system. Their world is filled with fantasy, and yours will be
too, if you make the effort to interact with them. Kindergarten
and primary-grade teachers score very well in creativity aptitude tests. One study showed that 58 percent of them rated
extremely high in imagination when compared to other occu-
pational groups.

One way to interact creatively with children is to play the
association game with them. The rules are simple. You both
look at something together and ask the child (or children),
"What does that look like to you?" or "What does that make
you think of?"

For example, you're outside and a formation of clouds is
passing over. "What figures do you see in the clouds,
Tommy?" Tommy replies, "I see a chocolate soda with
whipped cream on top. A large oak tree. A big frog. Two
horses. And Big Bird." Try to visualize them with him. (AU-
THOR'S NOTE: If Tommy answers, "I see cirrus and cumulus
formations," get yourself another kid for this exercise.) Once
you have visualized something together, make up a story
about it. Look at anything. Go through a picture book and
make up stories and captions. Stand on a mountaintop and ask
a child what the fields laid out in the valley look like. Colored
blocks? A quilt? A map?

In his book *Put Your Mother on the Ceiling*, Richard De
Mille has assembled a number of games that are designed to
exercise children's imaginations through directed imagery. In
each game, a parent, teacher, adult friend or teen-ager reads a
series of statements which the child is asked to visualize. At

the beginning of the game, each child is given a short introduction of what the game is about and told the name of the
game. At the end of the game he or she is asked to repeat the
name of the game. This signals to the child that it's time to
return to reality and that the game is ending. Through these
games De Mille is trying to exercise a child's imagination in
such a way that the child comes to realize that imagination and
reality can live in harmony. The following is the beginning,
ending and a few statements taken from one of the thirty
games in the book:

> Have you ever seen a live elephant as small as a mouse?
> Are there any real elephants that small in India or
> Africa, or at the zoo or the circus? I don't think so.
>
> This game is called ANIMALS.
>
> We are going to start with one little mouse and see
> what we can do.
>
> Let us imagine that there is a little mouse somewhere
> in the room. Where would you like to put him?/ All
> right, have him sit up and wave to you./ Have him turn
> green./ Change his color again./ Change it again./ Have
> him stand on his hands./ Have him run over to the wall./
> Have him run up the wall./ Have him sit upside down
> on the ceiling. (The game goes on for several pages.)
>
> What was the name of the game we just played?

Playing imagination games with children and creatively interacting with them is one good way to get you back in touch
with the imagination that you put in mothballs long ago. Another, similar set of visual imagery exercises is contained in
the book *Scamper, Games for Imagination and Development*
by Robert F. Eberle. Scamper games have been tested on all
ages from three years to adult and were found valuable in the
development of imagination.

Games and Puzzles

Certain games and puzzles can furnish you with plenty of
opportunity to flex your creative muscles. The games of chess
and checkers are both good examples. Both games force you

to map out strategies and make moves that depend on what your opponent does. Therefore, your success is determined by your ability to come up with new strategies and moves as the game develops.

Physical sports such as football, basketball, baseball, tennis, racketball or handball can also provide creative exercise. Frequently, the difference between winning and losing is to come up with a strategy that allows you to outwit your opponent. Good quarterbacks in football avoid trying to fall into a predictable pattern of calling plays. This gives them the edge of unpredictability and forces the defense to be prepared for anything. In his book *Bear*, Coach Bryant of Alabama recounts how he outwitted archrival Auburn. For some years he was beating Auburn using smaller, quicker players and then they tried to imitate him. As Bear put it, ". . . they were using those big burly boys and we beat 'em with little quick ones. They switched to the little quick ones and we went to the big ones and beat 'em some more. Now they're back to the big ones. It's flattering actually."

Most sports fans exercise their creative muscles while watching spectator sports on television or listening to them on radio. Try to guess what play the quarterback is calling in the huddle. What play would you call to take the defense by surprise? Map out an overall strategy for both teams before the game. Mentally involving yourself with the strategy of a game on television is far more beneficial than passively watching.

Charades is another game that provides great creative exercise. The person acting out his message is forced to think up novel ways to get it across. And trying to decipher the message calls for a large amount of thinking up too.

Word puzzles and games are another avenue for creative exercise and Thomas Edison was a great believer in this. Today, daily newspapers carry puzzles of the crossword and jumbled-word varieties. A great word game, such as Scrabble or Boggle, forces you to think in terms of adding, subtracting and modifying various combinations of letters, all of which helps sharpen and tone your creative ability.

Hobbies

Hobbies exist by the hundreds and some of them can be real workouts for your imagination. Painting, drawing or sculpture can't avoid putting your creative machinery to work. A gentleman in my neighborhood recently constructed a fenced-in landscape on the New Orleans lakefront from a collection of driftwood, bottles, shoes, and other debris that washed on shore. It's quite a work of art.

Woodworking, sewing, metalworking and numerous other crafts can be great diversions as well as creative exercise. Remember, these activities will give you the most exercise if you invent your own designs and carry them out.

For the more scientifically inclined, technical hobbies can provide creative exercise. Amateur radio buffs do a great deal more than communicate with other hams throughout the world and provide necessary communication during emergencies and disasters. Many of them design, test and build their own equipment. The result of this imagineering is that almost every technical breakthrough in electronic communication can be attributed to the work of radio amateurs. Hams have designed satellites which have been accepted into NASA programs. Others flash television pictures instantaneously to each other around the globe. Many of our best scientists, engineers and technicians have come to their chosen livelihood as a result of pursuing the hobby as a young person. Home computers is another technical hobby with great creative potential. The exercise in this hobby can be found in thinking up new uses for the computer in the home and writing new programs to carry them out. I have no doubt that future advances in computer technology will come in large part from the work of computer hobbyists.

Reading

Alex Osborn was a great believer in the value of reading as a creative exercise. He wrote, "Reading supplies bread for imagination to feed on, and bones for it to chew on." But, not all reading is good creative exercise. The key to using reading as a creative exercise is to read selectively and actively.

Reading selectively means choosing material that will provide a good workout for your imagination. Most novels offer little more than escapism, but a good mystery or short story can really get your creative juices flowing. One way to exercise your imagination with short stories is to read the first half and make up your own ending before reading the second half. In order to exercise his imagination, George Bernard Shaw would write an outline of each book he was about to read *before* he opened it.

Biographies also can be used for creative exercise. Any life worth documenting usually involved some real imagineering on the part of the subject. Perhaps you can profit from their experiences and use their creative ideas as a springboard to launch your own imagination. Many of our Presidents (such as Kennedy and Lincoln) were avid readers of biographies in their youth.

How-to books, be they cookbooks, repair manuals, self-help or whatever, can also be used for creative exercise. Take the ideas presented and see if you can improve them by adding, subtracting, modifying or combining them with new ideas of your own.

Another way to use reading as a creative exercise is to take a topic of interest and read several differing viewpoints. For example, if you're interested in writing a short story about the American Revolution, you would find it helpful to read the work of both American and British historians. And the viewpoints of French and Spanish historians could furnish a third and fourth perspective. The more points of view you can gain on any subject, the greater the odds that your own thought process will generate new ideas.

Magazines can also be used for creative exercise. Walt Disney believed in reading the *Reader's Digest* and said, "Your imagination may be creaky or timid or dwarfed or frozen at the points. The *Reader's Digest* can serve as a gymnasium for its training." One of the best things about *Reader's Digest* is that it provides a kaleidoscope of topics in every issue. Such diversity can provide great creative fuel.

Creative reading is best done by being an active reader. Read with a pencil or pen in your hand and underline key passages and take notes as you read. Read slowly, taking time to reflect on what you have read. In order to exercise your imagination you have to stop and think as you read. And the more you think about what you read, the greater are the odds that you'll generate new ideas.

Writing

About writing, Don Marquis remarked, "I never think when I write. Nobody can do two things at the same time and do them well." Actually, writing ability is considered to be a basic factor in creative aptitude. The act of writing forces you to utilize all phases of the creative process and come up with a tangible product.

You don't have to be a born writer in order to write as a creative exercise. Start by writing short pieces about a subject that interests or disturbs you. The essence of writing is to realize that it's mostly thinking. Start a short story with a real or imaginary incident and let your imagination wander. Who knows? Maybe you'll soon be writing for profit. For every best-selling author who breaks the bank, there are scores of others who supplement their regular incomes handsomely by writing. If you're serious about wanting to write and publish, read *How to Get Happily Published* by Nancy Evans and Judith Appelbaum. It's an outstanding book on the subject.

TECHNIQUES FOR GENERATING AND CAPTURING NEW IDEAS

Over the years, creative thinkers and problem solvers have come up with numerous gimmicks and gadgets for stimulating and capturing new ideas. The following are some of the more tried and true.

Use Checklists

The checklist approach to new ideas is a favorite technique of creative people. The idea is simple: Get a list of topics or words and consider them in light of the subject you are trying to think creatively about.

A very common and effective checklist was the one devised by Alex F. Osborn. The list consists of a number of verbs such as *magnify, minify, substitute, rearrange, reverse* and *combine*. The technique is to try and apply each of these verbs to the problem at hand in hopes of coming up with new ideas. For example, let's assume you're trying to do some innovating in your kitchen. You realize that your meal planning has fallen into a humdrum routine. Armed with a checklist of verbs, you begin to consider future meals and start generating ideas. The word *magnify* brings some ideas to light:

1. Plan more meals of an ethnic variety.
2. Add more seafood to the meals.
3. Have at least two new dishes a week.

The verb *minify* reminds you to reduce the number of starches in the meal. *Rearrange* reminds you to stop serving the same dish for Sunday dinner and so on.

In order to use the checklist technique you don't have to go to the trouble of having or making a checklist. For example, paging through the table of contents of magazines can give a writer numerous ideas about what to write on. Someone in search of a new career can page through the Yellow Pages of the telephone directory and come up with plenty of possibilities to explore. Paging through an issue of *National Geographic* can serve as an idea generator for deciding where to take your next vacation. Although this technique may not get you initially what you seek as a satisfactory solution, it's one of the methods you can use to get yourself producing ideas.

Forced Relationships Can Help

Another idea-producing technique is to try and force a relationship between two previously unrelated ideas or things. The result is often a new product or idea. Mickey Mouse watches and combination electric can opener-juicers are examples of forced-relationship products. How about a restaurant made out of railroad boxcars? That's what Victoria Station restaurants are constructed from.

Forced relationships are usually established by arbitrary

and mechanical means. For example, a favorite technique of creative people is to have a container of idea starters. If your job is to write advertising copy, begin collecting old advertisements, clippings, ideas and designs. When you have a new ad to write, shake up the box of ideas and pull out two or more at random. See if these ideas can be combined and applied to the problem at hand. If the answer is no, put the starters back in the box, shake them up and pull two more. Eventually, you'll come up with a useful combination of ideas.

New ideas for products can also be spawned by forcing relationships. My friend Denny Had, president of Dentron Radio, has profited handsomely by combining two or more products to produce a third product. In one instance he took an antenna tuner, watt meter, dummy antenna and combined them into one product. The old products separately sold for $359, but the combination was sold for $349. However, the profit margin on the combination product was much greater because of lower labor and materials cost. If you're in business, make a list of all your products and services. Choose two or more at random and see if you can come up with another product or service. Browse through your catalog and see if you can come up with any new ideas by forcing relationships. It can be very profitable.

List Attributes

Attribute listing is a special form of the checklist technique. In this case, the idea seeker lists all the various attributes of the thing he or she wishes to think about.

Attention is then turned specifically to each one of the attributes, which is used as a checklist for thinking up new ideas. One common example of this is to consider the attributes of a common wooden-handle screwdriver. We begin by listing its attributes: 1) round, 2) steel shaft, 3) wooden handle, 4) wedge-shaped tip, 5) manually operated and 6) torque provided by twisting action.

To design a better screwdriver, you then focus on each attribute separately. Could the round shaft be made hexagonal so that a wrench could be used for turning with greater torque? What if we remove the wooden handle and design the shaft to fit an electric drill? This gives us a power tool. What if we make several interchangeable shafts for different size screws? The basic premise of attribute listing is to look at each component and ask "Why does this have to be this way?" "How can this be done differently?" It's a great way of breaking us out of unconscious conceptual assumptions.

Use the Morphological Approach

The morphological approach to generating new ideas is one of the few things in life that's easier done than said. Basically, this technique combines attribute listing with forced relationships, and the result is the speedy production of a tremendous number of ideas.

This technique is best described by example. Let's suppose you're a television programing executive and you're trying to come up with some novel ideas for programing that will improve your ratings. You first begin listing some of the attributes of television programing such as days, times, target audience, type of show and sponsor. Then under each heading you list several alternatives, and the result is a matrix which might look like this:

Type of Show	Target Audience	Airing Day	Airing Time	Sponsor
News	Preschool children	Sunday	6-7 A.M.	Oil
Sports	School-age children	Monday	7-9 A.M.	Automobile
Drama	Teens	Tuesday	9 A.M.-12 Noon	Cosmetics
Sit-Com	Housewives	Wednesday	12-3 P.M.	Pharmaceuticals
Musical	Men	Thursday	3-7 P.M.	Clothing
Documentary	Women	Friday	7-11 P.M.	Real Estate
Talk Show	Senior Citizens	Saturday	After 11 P.M.	Cereal

The next step is to choose one or more items from each of the headings at random and connect them to form a novel idea for a new show. You now have the potential to generate countless thousands of ideas for new shows. How about a sit-com for housewives and senior citizens airing on Tuesday mornings between 9 A.M. and noon sponsored by a pharmaceutical company?

The advantage of the morphological approach and the previous techniques is that it helps break us out of habitual patterns of thinking. It's important to realize that the ideas created by these techniques are often just a starting point in the creative process. It usually takes a lot of trying, refining and developing to come up with a workable idea.

Set Deadlines and Quotas

The importance of setting deadlines was discussed earlier. In addition to promising yourself ideas by a certain time, set a quota of ideas to be thought up. Tell yourself, "I'll come up with thirty-five new ideas for——by this time next week." Better yet, write it down. That may sound like a large quota of ideas, but it's only five new ideas per day for a week. The first five will likely be the hardest to generate and then they will trigger other ideas. And the more ideas you gather, the better the chances of coming up with an answer you're looking for.

Carry Index Cards or a Pocket Recorder

Ralph Waldo Emerson wrote: "Look sharply after your thoughts. They come unlooked for, like a new bird seen in your trees, and, if you turn to your usual task, disappear." Ideas are thoughts and thoughts are fleeting. Unless you make the effort to document your ideas, you'll lose many of them in the shuffle of day-to-day activity. There's absolutely no way to predict when a great idea is likely to pop into your mind. Therefore, the only way to reduce the risk of losing it is to be prepared at all times. Carry a notepad or some small index cards and a pen or pencil with you at all times. Better yet get one of the handheld microcassette recorders. When that new idea comes, get it on paper or tape. This technique is absolutely indispensable to me as a writer. You can't begin to imagine how many good ideas you have until you begin to document them. And as you read them over, these ideas, in turn, trigger more ideas.

Pulitzer prize-winning author Dr. Carl Sagan stated in an

interview that he carries a cassette recorder everywhere he goes. As Sagan put it. he sits down and writes whenever he hears "the rap on the door." "Sometimes the rap is polite and other times it is very insistent. Generally speaking, I find my-self caught up in a passion, some sort of excitement, and I sit down and write. I often do the first draft by dictating it into a cassette recorder I carry around with me everywhere. Some-times I'll be sitting on an airplane, and I hear a whole chapter knocking on the door, waiting to come out."

Whether you use a notepad, index cards, cassette recorder or whatever, always carry something with you that will enable you to record your ideas.

Get Yourself an Idea Bank

Another favorite technique of idea people is to have a central place to store ideas that relate to a particular subject. The idea bank can be a file folder, shoe box, desk drawer or whatever. Whenever you have a good idea, write it down and bank it. Also, anything you run across such as clippings, cartoons, quotes, pictures or helpful hints can be stored in the idea bank. When you get ready to start some serious imagineering, you'll have a large number of previous ideas to get you started.

Set Aside a Definite Time and Place

New ideas can also be induced by setting aside a certain time and place for thinking up. All of us are creatures of habit. If you consciously choose a particular time and place for inno-vating, you'll find that ideas will start to come almost auto-matically as you cultivate the habit. At first ideas may come slowly, and some days you may come away without any new ideas. Just be persistent. As author Flannery O'Connor put it, "Many times I just sit for three hours with no ideas coming to me. But I know one thing: if an idea does come between nine and twelve, I am there ready for it." Be sure to choose a quiet place that isolates you from interruptions and distractions and where you can be alone with your thoughts for several hours at a time.

Sleep and Think Up

One favorite technique of many innovators is this: Always keep a notepad and pencil at your bedside. Illumination frequently sneaks up on us in the middle of the night. If you're working on a problem, write down what's blocking your progress, forget it and go to sleep. Often you will awaken with a myriad of new ideas and solutions. If you awaken in the night with a great idea, write it down before it slips away. Of course, you can also use a cassette recorder in lieu of the pencil and pad. Short daytime naps can also help bring about new ideas. This was one of Thomas Edison's favorite techniques for problem solving. Don't resist your natural urge to get away from the problem. Let your subconscious work on it.

Insomnia can also be put to creative use. Instead of worrying why you can't sleep, or counting sheep, pick an area in which you can generate some new ideas to help you achieve your goals. Who knows? You may come up with a very profitable idea. And thinking up will often bring about sleep.

Combine Creative Thinking with Routine Activities

Much of our daily living consists of routine, sometimes boring activities that require little or no mental effort on our part. Why not put this time to a second use? Be creative and think up.

House and yard work are excellent candidates. If we choose something to think about, the tedium of these activities will be diminished and the time will seem to pass faster.

Walking, running and cycling are great for creative thinking. Since the days of Thoreau, taking walks has been a favorite way to court new ideas. Going for a walk through a shopping center or downtown business district can put us in contact with all sorts of new stimuli to spark our imaginations. Or a quiet walk in the woods can provide the tranquil solitude necessary to come up with a satisfactory solution to a problem. Cycling and running can provide the relaxed frame of mind necessary for creating new ideas. Similarly, many people report gaining some of their greatest insights while walking on golf courses.

Bathtubs are great places for ideas. The most famous example of this concerns Archimedes. He was faced with the task of finding out whether or not a crown was pure gold. How to determine the cubic area of the crown puzzled him. So he tried taking a hot bath to spur his creative thinking. I'll let him tell the rest:

"My body makes the water rise. It displaces exactly the same cubic area. I will immerse the crown in water, measure how much it displaces, and thus find its cubic area. Multiplying that by the known weight of gold, I can then prove whether the crown is a counterfeit. *Eureka!*"

Whether showering, shaving or bathing, many people claim to do their best creative thinking in bathrooms. One good reason for this is probably because they're isolated from distracting influences.

Much of our time is also taken up with waiting and commuting. Like the other mundane activities, they can be made more pleasant by having something ready for our imaginations to work on as we pass the time. One advertising agency executive uses commuting time to think up and record ideas for upcoming campaigns. Sales representatives can use traveling and waiting time to think up new benefits and approaches to selling their goods and services. By making the effort to think, wasted moments can become immediately productive. Whenever you're at a loss for something to do, think "think up." And have several projects ready for your imagination to work on.

How to Keep the Flow of New Ideas Coming

As I noted earlier, the production of new ideas is enhanced by suspending judgment. Never try to think up new ideas and evaluate them at the same time. First think up, then evaluate. As you imagineer, think of yourself as two people: at one time a thinker-upper and at another time a judge. Only evaluate your ideas after you've exhausted your idea-producing capabilities. This will increase the number of ideas you think up, and the greater the number of ideas, the better are the chances of coming up with an excellent one. As Frank Tyger put it, "Success is often just an idea away."

4

Team Up for Super Imagineering

*"There are two ways of spreading light: to be the candle,
or the mirror that reflects it."*

—Edith Wharton

OLIVER WENDELL HOLMES once remarked, "Many ideas grow better when transplanted into another mind than in the one where they sprang up." Modern science, business and technology have heeded his words. The breakthroughs and innovations of tinkerers, shade-tree thinkers and rugged individualists have given way to massive group efforts requiring big money and complex research facilities. The task of putting a man on the moon took the creative effort of millions. Contrast this with the fact that only two men were responsible for the invention of the airplane. Corporations, universities and governments spend billions each year on research and development. All these phenomena are an outgrowth of one simple belief: *Thinking up is better when you team up.*

You don't have to be a scientist or researcher to reap the benefits of team creativity. Joint ideation can be used to solve problems in a small business, a family, in church groups, on vacations or wherever there happens to be more than one person involved. Teaming up can improve the morale of individuals by soliciting their ideas. It can provide more and better ideas if properly used. It can bring people closer and improve communication. And it can also be a lot of fun. In this chapter, we will examine some of the more basic techniques used in group creativity and show how they can be applied to the problems of daily living.

INDIVIDUAL CREATIVITY STILL COUNTS MOST

The first and foremost rule of group creativity is to recognize that it is a supplement and not a substitute for individual creativity. Joint creative strategies were not designed with the intent of replacing individual effort. Despite whatever advances have been the products of organized research and group thinking, the creative power of the individual still counts most. Dr. Ernest Benger of the DuPont research staff wisely embodied this philosophy. Said Dr. Benger, "No idea has ever been generated except in a single human mind. . . . No matter how you toss this thought around or how you add to it by consideration of the effect of getting people into a coordinated organization, the fact remains that every idea is the product of a single brain."

In some situations, group problem-solving approaches can be a waste of time. When people are indifferent about participating, it's a waste of time. When the problem is very broad, the value of these techniques is questionable. Some people have an intense level of motivation and temperament that allows them to produce better ideas than any group could begin to hope for. Robert Koch singularly is credited as the man who isolated bacteria by types. And it's difficult to imagine such creative classics as Michelangelo's *Moses*, Shakespeare's *Macbeth*, or Beethoven's Ninth Symphony being created by more than one person.

However, in many situations, group ideation techniques can provide plenty of new ideas to spur the efforts of individual creativity. Let's look at a few.

THE TWO-PERSON CREATIVE TECHNIQUE

Thomas Carlyle wrote, "The lightning spark of thought generated in the solitary mind awakens its likeness in another mind." Creative twosomes are a favorite of the music business. One writes the words and another the music. Rodgers and Hammerstein is a case in point. Comedy writers frequently work in twosomes. Their good-natured spontaneity can be mutually contagious.

When I wrote and produced radio commercials with a partner, our best ideas came spontaneously as we worked in a spirit of fun. Turning on a tape recorder, Andy and I would first begin casually discussing the spot we had to make. Who was it for? How long should it be? What would be a good angle? Current events? A political figure? A cartoon character? Informally defining the problem spurred and channeled our creative efforts. Soon ideas would be pouring out of us at a rapid pace. After exhausting our ideas, we would go back and listen to the tape. Often, we could edit a spot directly from the tape. We were never at a loss for ideas.

Most of us can produce better ideas if we are teamed up with the right partner. Team up with an incompatible partner and you've got a creative wasteland. A good partner tends to spur effort as well as our powers of association. The following guidelines are very helpful for creative twosomes. They will ensure that you get the best combination of individual and joint effort.

1. Be Sure There's an Incentive for Both of You

There has to be something in it that will make the investment of time and effort in thinking up a worthwhile endeavor for everyone. Otherwise that all-important drive to spur ideas will not be present. If you don't do this, two heads won't be better than one. They'll just be thicker. Also be sure that the incentives for you both are compatible and not at odds with each other.

2. Choose a Time and Place to Think

Once you and your partner have a topic that requires mutual creative effort, the next step is to choose a future time and place for creative thought. This will allow both of you time to think alone about the problem. If necessary, you can gather information or let the problem incubate in your subconscious.

As an example, let's assume that you and your spouse have decided to build or buy a house. You decide that next Tuesday evening from seven until eight you'll meet and generate ideas for the home of your dreams. Between now and then you can think about what each of you needs or wants in a new house in terms of size, proximity to schools and work, furnishings, access to transportation and any other factors you would like to consider. You also can gather information by reading books and magazines on the subjects of home building and furnishing. You both have time to fuel your idea machines.

3. Meet and Think Together

Be sure to make this a fun exercise. Keep it informal as you bounce your ideas off each other. This informal and accepting atmosphere will keep the flow of new ideas coming. Be sure to consider every idea that's mentioned. This isn't the time or place to say "I don't like that idea" or "That won't work." Go for a quantity of ideas and get them all in writing. Have a cassette recording your ideas, in case you miss one or forget it before having a chance to write it down.

4. Think Alone

Now that you've both had the benefit of thinking up together, go back and consider the problem by yourself. This gives you the benefit of thinking alone after having thought as a team. This often results in newer and better ideas.

5. Meet Again and Choose a Satisfactory Solution

First, take any new ideas thought of alone and add them to ideas thought up at the first meeting. The last and final step is to begin choosing mutually satisfactory alternatives. Now is the time to bring in judgment, tastes, preferences and the like. The refinement and evaluation of these alternatives will likely result in a workable idea.

Going back to our home-buying example, let's assume that both of you generated a total of one hundred ideas on what features you would like in your new house. The next step might be to go down the list and scratch off those items that would be too costly or unfeasible. Then each of you can rank the remaining ideas on the list in order of personal preference. You now have a criteria for buying or building a house that will accommodate both your needs.

6. Refrain from Destructive Arguing

No matter what stage of the two-person creative process you're in, the worst thing you can do is argue with each other. This will destroy the climate necessary to keep the flow of ideas coming. Many potentially good ideas will be destroyed in the embryonic stage if an atmosphere of argument prevails. This doesn't mean that ideas can't be intelligently discussed in the judgment stage. However, the implied message in any argument is that one person is right and the other is wrong. Creativity and criticism are incompatible. As Robert Quillen put it, "Discussion is an exchange of knowledge, argument is an exchange of ignorance."

ANYONE FOR BRAINSTORMING?

Brainstorming is the most well known and used of the group creativity techniques. It's even listed in *Webster's New World Dictionary* and defined there as "the unrestrained offering of ideas or suggestions by all members of a group meeting as in a business planning conference." The concept was popularized by Alex Osborn, who first utilized the technique in 1938. The term *brainstorm* came from the idea of using the brain to storm a problem. The concept of brainstorming was not totally new in 1938. A similar procedure has been practiced by Hindu teachers in India for more than four hundred years.

A brainstorming session is simply a creative meeting whose single purpose is to produce a checklist of ideas which can *later* be evaluated and processed as possible solutions to problems. Brainstorming became very popular in the 1950s, after which its popularity faded fast. However, its problems were due mainly to a misunderstanding of the brainstorming process and failure to recognize its limitations. Brainstorming is not a panacea or magical solution to problems. It's merely one tool that can be used in one part of the creative problem-solving process, and that's all it ever was intended to be.

The creative problem-solving process can be summarized in three steps:

1. Fact finding—gathering information about the problem (preparation)
2. Idea finding—thinking up alternative solutions to the problem (illumination)
3. Solution finding—refining, verifying ideas and choosing the best alternative idea or ideas

Brainstorming is merely one tool that can be used to generate ideas in the idea-finding stage. These ideas have to be *later* evaluated as a basis for problem solving. (The evaluation of ideas is covered in Chapter Six.)

The greatest value of brainstorming is that it can provide more good ideas than a conventional meeting and in less time. Most of us are all too familiar with the typical committee meeting which is rarely a vehicle for creativity. A plaque on my office wall sums it up nicely: "God so loved the world that he didn't send a committee."

Brainstorming has a wide range of applicability as an idea-generating technique. The following are instances in which this technique was used successfully. These testimonials are reported by Alex Osborn in his book *Applied Imagination*.

1. Argus Camera conducted three brainstorm sessions to find potential ways to economize on purchasing. Ideas were generated that were immediately usable and could result in a savings of $46,000 a year.
2. The Swiss Society of Life Insurance brainstormed 225 new ideas on the topic of how to find new salesmen. Twenty-five were later found worthy of immediate adoption and 125 were potentially usable.
3. A group of executives brainstormed the problem of what

to do about the engineering shortage. In twenty-five minutes they produced 110 ideas, and 6 were found to be worthy of adoption.

4. A Catholic community church in France came up with 385 ideas in answer to the problem of how to make their community more livable. Seventy of these ideas were found to be usable.

5. The Cleveland Advertising Club brainstormed the problem of ways to publicize Opera Week and get as many people as possible to buy tickets. Out of a total of 124 ideas suggested, 29 were implemented, and the seats at the opera were filled.

6. A movie producer lived with his parents and five unmarried brothers. Family squabbles and disharmony were the norm. He organized the family into a brainstorming group and tackled family problems one at a time. He reported: "Some of our ideas worked and improved the harmony of our home. Much to our surprise, we all had a lot of fun at these sessions."

Brainstorming Rules and Guidelines

There are four simple, basic rules to any brainstorming conference:

1. *Judgment and criticism are forbidden*. As one brainstorming group leader explained: "If you try to get hot and cold water out of the same faucet at the same time, you will only get tepid water. And if you try to criticize and create at the same time, you can't turn on either *cold* enough criticism or *hot* enough ideas. So let's stick solely to *ideas*—let's cut out *all* criticism *during* this session." People who insist on criticizing should be gently warned, and if that doesn't work they should be firmly stopped. Tell them to think up or shut up.

2. *"Freewheeling" is welcoming*. As Osborn puts it, "The wilder the idea, the better; it is easier to tame down than to think up."

3. *Go for quantity*. The greater the number of ideas, the greater are the odds of finding a useful idea.

4. *Seek to combine and improve ideas as they are mentioned.* People should try to improve each other's ideas as well as think up new ideas of their own.

In addition to the four basic rules, you should be aware of the following guidelines if you're considering using brainstorming as an idea-finding technique.

1. The problem to be brainstormed should be specific rather than general. This will allow participants to concentrate their efforts on a single topic. Try to keep the problem as simple as possible. The more complicated a problem is, the more difficult it will be to focus group effort on a single target.

If you're trying to brainstorm something like how to improve employee productivity in an organization, this is too broad a topic. The problem must be broken into segments. Begin by considering how to improve productivity in sales, distribution, finance, personnel and various other organizational divisions or departments. Then try brainstorming specific problem areas for each department, such as how to reduce absenteeism in finance or turnover in sales representatives or how to better evaluate employees in personnel. The main idea is to narrow the problem sufficiently and specifically enough to enable the group to home in their ideation efforts in an effective manner.

2. Only use brainstorming for problems that call for idea finding rather than judgment. Problems having a narrow and limited number of options aren't suitable for brainstorming. For example, problems such as whether or not to go to college, whether to take a new job offer or whether to buy or rent aren't suitable for brainstorming. Problems such as these require judgment. One good way to handle these types of problems is the balance-sheet approach. List all of the pros and cons of each alternative and choose the one that appears the most satisfactory.

3. Once a problem has been defined and deemed suitable for brainstorming, circulate a memo to participants stating the time and place where the meeting will be held. In this memo, be sure to highlight the problem and give several examples of the types of ideas to be thought up. This will prepare people

so they will know that this isn't going to be a conventional meeting. Osborn recommends that the ideal number of people for a brainstorming session is twelve and that the meeting should last approximately thirty minutes.

4. Begin the brainstorming session by explaining the four basic rules. It's a good idea to write them on a chalkboard, or better yet, have a placard made stating the four rules. This can be displayed as a visual aid throughout the meeting.

5. Take pains to avoid an atmosphere of perfectionism. Keep the atmosphere informal and funlike. Promote a spirit of friendly rivalry among the group. You want the type of spirit that could well be found at a party or picnic game.

6. Be sure to encourage ideas that are sparked by previous ideas. The objective is to get a chain reaction going where participants are creatively feeding off of each other.

7. Have a nonparticipant present to record every idea that is mentioned.

Why It Works

The high productivity of ideas in brainstorming sessions has been documented many times over. Yet it seems only reasonable to ask "Why is it so effective?" There are several reasons.

First, the power of associating ideas provides a two-way current. Whenever someone states a new idea, he stirs his own imagination as well as everyone else's. As one participant remarked, "When you really get going in a brainstorm session, a spark from one mind will light up a lot of bang-up ideas in the others just like a string of firecrackers." This chain reaction value of brainstorming is the reason most frequently given for its effectiveness.

Another reason this technique is effective is due to what is called *social facilitation*. All it means is that people tend to think up more ideas in the presence of other people than they do alone. Tests of free associations have shown adults produce from 65 to 93 percent more ideas in group activity than when thinking alone.

As I pointed out earlier, creativity depends more on motivation and mental effort than any other factor. A brainstorming session can provide this motivation by having people compete to think of ideas. Psychologists have shown that mental output can be increased by an amount of 50 percent or more when stirred by competition.

Finally, brainstorming is effective because it reinforces (rewards) the behavior of the participants by completely accepting all ideas. Most conventional meetings are fraught with an atmosphere of judgment and criticism. This negative reinforcement tends to inhibit the production of new ideas. Because brainstorming accepts all ideas, it rules out the possibility of any premature judgment or criticism. The behavior of producing new ideas is rewarded by its acceptance, and rewarded behavior tends to be repeated.

New Twists

Leaders of brainstorm sessions have tried numerous gimmicks and gadgets to increase the rate of idea production. Three that I'm familiar with are worthy of mentioning.

"Stop-and-go" brainstorming is one variation that has been practiced for some time. The rules are the same except the session is broken into segments. After the rules are explained, the leader allows the group to think up and spurt out ideas for three minutes. Then the group stops and there is a five-minute period of silence for incubation. Then there is another three-minute drive for new ideas, five minutes of silence, three minutes of thinking up, and so on.

The sequencing procedure is another technique that can be added. The rules are the same as conventional brainstorming with one exception. Instead of shouting out ideas in a spontaneous, random fashion, each member takes turns at giving out what ideas he has at the time. If he has no ideas, he simply passes to the next person. Ideas are solicited on a roundtable basis until the session is over. Thomas Bouchard, who is credited with carrying out numerous experiments comparing sequencing-procedure brainstorming to conventional brainstorming, reported that his groups produced 87.5 percent more ideas using the sequencing procedure.

A third twist to conventional brainstorming is the Phillips 66 buzz session developed by Donald Phillips. The buzz session combines brainstorming with group competition and provides a method for using larger numbers of people than would be feasible for ordinary brainstorming. A large number of people are divided into small groups, and each group has a chairperson who is briefed beforehand on brainstorming techniques. Each small group is instructed to brainstorm the same problem in the conventional manner. After brainstorming, each group selects the best idea or best several ideas, which the group leader then presents to the rest of the groups. The advantage of this technique lies in its applicability to a large number of people. However, it has the disadvantage of calling for evaluation and judgment of ideas at a very early stage. Some good ideas may be prematurely screened out and never be given any serious consideration.

SYNETICS—the Use of Analogies

Aristotle remarked, "The greatest thing by far is to be master of the metaphor." When I first began writing, I read a passage that said good writers know how to make new things seem familiar and familiar things seem new. This approach to creativity is the backbone of a very popular group problem-solving technique called *synetics*.

Synetics group sessions take a very structural approach to harnessing group creativity. The role for the leader in the group is not to act as a judge, moderator or chairman. His sole function is to ensure that the problem being investigated is kept within the confines of a lengthy flow chart of steps in the process.

The synetics technique is a rather involved one and outside of the scope and purpose of this book. If you're interested in synetics as a technique, I suggest reading *The Practice of Creativity* by George Prince or *Synetics* by William J. J. Gordon.

What we can learn from synetics and practice as groups or as individuals is the important use of analogies in creative thinking.

Making the Strange Familiar

By nature, all of us are conservative and have a tendency to feel threatened by the unfamiliar. Consequently, one of the first things we do when confronted with a new concept or thing is to try and perceive it in a familiar light. We tend to familiarize by using two techniques.

One method is to analyze. We take the new phenomenon and break it down into as many parts as we can and study them individually. In high school we learned the anatomy of a frog by dissecting and discovering its component parts and biological systems and how they are related to one another. As we began to understand how each component functioned, we understood more about the whole frog and how it functioned. Analysis is one way of making the strange familiar.

Another approach to familiarizing is to generalize via analogy. In effect, we ask ourselves, "What's this like?" Analogy is a tremendous teaching tool. Persons teaching basic electricity frequently use the analogy of water flowing through pipes from a water tower to explain concepts of current, resistance and voltage. Many of the concepts learned from studying the anatomy of, a frog can be transferred to understanding the anatomy of higher animals and humans.

The process of making the strange familiar is most useful in the preparation stage of creativity. It provides us with a way of becoming comfortable with new ideas, things and problems. This sets the stage for the other phases of the process.

Making the Familiar Strange

Research in synetics has revealed that the ability to look at the same old thing in a brand new way is the key element to creative problem solving and innovating. Long before there was synetics, William James remarked, "Genius in truth means little more than the faculty of perceiving in an unhabitual way." Einstein's theory that matter could be converted into energy was a new way of looking at two very familiar phenomena. Likewise, when Columbus theorized the world was round and Copernicus stated that the earth was not the center of the universe, they exploded habitual popular concepts about the world and universe.

Whenever you're confronted with a problem or situation calling for creativity you must try and view it from a different perspective. Just as making the strange familiar helps with preparation, making the familiar strange is the key to illumination. The following quotes can best illustrate the concept of gaining a new perspective:

From the hayloft, a horse looks like a violin.

—*Lord Chesterfield*

A hen is only an egg's way of making another egg.

—*Samuel Butler*

Man—a creature made at the end of the week's work when God was tired.

—*Mark Twain*

Xerox: A trademark for a photocopying device that can make rapid reproductions of human error, perfectly.

Merle L. Meacham

Zoo: An excellent place to study the habits of human beings.

—*Evan Esar*

My uncle is a Southern planter. He's an undertaker in Alabama.

—*Fred Allen*

How does one go about thinking up, using analogies? Synetics uses the following four metaphorical techniques.

Direct Analogy or Model Building

When Lord Rutherford was trying to formulate a model to describe his theory of the atom, he constructed it to look like a miniature solar system. Many of the components of a camera parallel parts of the eye. Alexander Graham Bell conceived the telephone by modeling it after the human ear. As Bell put it: "It struck me that the bones of the human ear were very massive, indeed, as compared with the delicate thin membrane that operated them, and the thought occurred that if a membrane so delicate could move bones relatively so massive, why should not a thicker and stouter piece of membrane move any piece of steel. And the telephone was conceived." All of these are examples of creating a new idea or thing that directly parallels an existing one. That is the essence of a direct analogy.

Direct analogy is the most common type of analogy. You apply it by searching your own experiences and knowledge for a similar phenomenon or process that can be adapted to the problem at hand. The 3M Company went from producing sandpaper to roofing materials, to transparent tape, to magnetic tape, to photocopying, to reflective signs. The direct analogy here is that all these products require one common skill—how to apply a closely controlled layer of material on a flexible base.

Personal Analogy—Look, Ma, I'm a Radish

A personal analogy is basically role playing. You imagine yourself to be the person or thing being studied (or a part of it) and try to get a different view of the problem. It's an attempt to gain empathy. For example, some scientists try to gain technical insight into a problem by imagining themselves as dancing molecules or electrons. Artists as well as scientists have creatively benefited from using personal analogy. Keats, when discussing his writing of *Endymion*, said, "I leaped headlong into the sea and thereby have become better acquainted with the sounds, the quicksands and the rocks, than if I had stayed upon the green shore and piped a silly pipe and took tea and comfortable advice."

Personal analogy has tremendous potential for solving daily problems in our lives. Sales representatives can try to place themselves in the role of their customers and ask themselves, "If we were they, what would convince us to buy?" A manager trying to motivate an employee may come up with new ideas by trying to place himself in the employee's shoes.

Marriage and family counselors sometimes use role-playing exercises for resolving conflicts. Each person is asked to assume the role for the other in order to enable the combatants to understand each other's point of view. The value of empathy in any kind of interpersonal relationship cannot be underestimated, and it can serve as a vehicle for resolving many types of problems.

Symbolic Analogy

A symbolic analogy is a representation of the key elements of a problem as *you* see it. It's expressed in the form of an objective and impersonal image. It differs from the direct analogy in that it needn't be technically accurate.

In *Synetics*, Gordon illustrated how the following problem was solved through the use of symbolic analogies: "How to invent a jacking mechanism to fit a box not bigger than four by four inches yet extend out and up three feet and support four tons." The solution started to develop when someone suggested the Indian rope trick as a symbolic analogy. He remarked, "The rope is soft when the guy starts with it . . . the magic is how he makes it hard so he can climb up on it. . . ." Several other symbolic analogies were suggested by other members: the hydraulic principle of erection of the penis, an analogy of a steel tape measure, then to a bicycle chain with flexible links that stiffened as they were driven out of the jacking mechanism. Symbolic analogies were employed to look at jacks in a new way, and a successfully functioning jack was built that solved the problem.

Fantasy Analogy

As the old song goes, "Would you like to swing on a star or carry moonbeams home in a jar?" This is the essence of a fantasy analogy. To use fantasy analogy you state a problem in terms of how you wish things could be rather than how they actually are. Many of our greatest scientific and technical breakthroughs have their roots in fantasy analogies. No doubt, aviation is one of them, and for hundreds of years people wondered what it would be like if men could fly. This fantasy led to numerous attempts to put wings on men or get them airborne in some way and culminated with the invention of the airplane. Fantasy analogy can help by making familiar things seem new. Additionally, the wild fantasy of someone's imagination may spark a realistic idea in someone else's mind.

In summary, the use of analogies and metaphors gives us the ability to look at old things in new ways and new things in old ways. This is one very important facet of creative thinking.

HOW ABOUT A CREATIVE BULLETIN BOARD?

Have you ever considered using a bulletin board as a place to gather creative ideas and solutions to problems? Businesses, civic groups and families have successfully used memo boards as tools for creative problem solving. In its simplest form, the problem to be solved is written on a colored piece of paper or card and placed on the board for all interested parties to see. Anyone with an idea simply writes it on a white piece of paper or card and places it under the problem on the board.

This technique has several advantages. Like brainstorming, it can spur ideas by association. As one person reads the problem and ideas on the board, he will likely think of a new idea to contribute. Another advantage is that the problem can be left up for an indefinite period of time, giving people ample time to think about it. A final advantage is that it doesn't require everyone to be at a certain place at a certain time in order to contribute to thinking up ideas. Boards can be useful alternatives to calling a meeting. And anything that will reduce the number of meetings can't be all bad.

The next time you're searching for new ideas, team up and think up. No matter which techniques you use, you'll benefit by thinking up more ideas than you would have alone. Additionally, you'll reap a multitude of ideas from your teammates. It's a classic case of synergy in action.

5

Ask Questions to Spark Your Imagination

"Questions are the creative acts of intelligence."

—Frank Kingdon

THE STORY GOES that a father and his young son were walking down the street one day. The boy asked how electricity went through the wires overhead. "Don't know," said the father. "Never knew much about electricity." A short time later the boy asked what caused lightning and thunder. "To tell the truth, I never exactly understood that myself," said the father. A few more minutes passed and the son thought of another question. "Say, Pop, uh, never mind." "Go ahead. Ask questions," replied his father. "How else are you going to learn?"

THE QUESTION TECHNIQUE

Questions have been used as learning aids since the days of Socrates. What happens when someone asks you a question? You have to think about it. And if someone asks the right question, you have to think up, as well as think about something. As William A. Ward remarked, "Curiosity is the wick in the candle of learning."

Questions induce imagination. What if everyone had X-ray eyes? What if the moon was accessible on a commuter basis? Questions such as these can start our imaginations off in many different directions.

Practical creativity and problem solving also calls for asking questions. The key to making this technique an effective idea producer is to ask the right questions.

The questioning technique consists of two very simple steps:

1. Isolate the subject or problem you want to think about.
2. Ask a series of questions about each step of the subject or problem.

If you're armed with the right battery of questions, this technique will have you turning out new ideas at a very lively rate. In addition, these questions will cause you to think of many ideas that you wouldn't have considered without asking them.

The following questions are designed to spark ideation. The value of each question is explained with an anecdote that will demonstrate the question's utility. As you will soon see, some of these ideas, discoveries and inventions have made a greater contribution to mankind than others.

What Can Be Added?

Every good cook knows the value of this creative question. A clove of garlic here or a dash of sherry there can turn an otherwise plain dish into a gourmet's delight.

By accident, it was found that sandwiching a piece of plastic between two pieces of glass added strength to glass, resulting in shatterproof glass. The story goes that a chemist tipped over and broke a bottle containing a plastic substance called collodion. When he picked up the pieces of glass, he noticed that they stuck together. This lucky discovery led to the idea of laminating plastic with glass—an idea that no doubt has saved many lives and prevented numerous injuries.

Adding features to products or new products to a product line are very possible ideas that can come from asking this question. Every year new autos, appliances, watches and calculators appear with additional features. Homes and offices can be made more pleasant by adding the right environmental extras. By asking what can be added, the generation of new ideas is inevitable.

What If This Were Exaggerated?

Exaggeration is a favorite technique of creative people. A caricaturist or cartoonist exaggerates the features of their subjects. Satire is an exaggeration of an existing situation.

Carrying things to the point of exaggeration doesn't necessarily mean making things bigger. For example, in 1853, George Crum, an Adirondack Indian chief, was employed as a head chef at a posh resort in New York State. One evening, a guest kept repeatedly sending his french fries back to the kitchen, complaining they were too thick. In a rage, Crum picked up his knife, sliced a potato into paper thin pieces and dropped them into boiling fat. He then personally served them to the malcontent guest, who proclaimed them to be delicious. The potato chip had been born. Today it's estimated that the average American consumes over thirteen pounds of chips each year.

What Else Can This Be Used For?

Finding new uses for old things is another great creative technique. A recent helpful-hints book was full of ideas for new applications of existing things: using hairspray to remove a ballpoint-ink stain and an electric shaver to remove fuzz balls from old shirt collars. The book even recommended cleaning eyeglasses with vodka! That should do wonders for anyone's outlook.

Some people have gone from rags to riches by finding new uses for existing things. A man named Bob Brown is one of them. In 1971 Brown, a polio victim, was living on Social Security. One day while assembling an electric guitar in his garage, he accidentally crossed some wires and a group of observing rats panicked and fled for their lives. Realizing what he had done, Brown applied the idea and built a "rat repellent box." The box generates a signal at one million cycles per second, which is far out of the range of the human ear. However, it reportedly has a deleterious effect on rats, cockroaches and ants. "We're jamming the sensory systems of rats, cockroaches and even ants like a foreign broadcaster jams our radios," said Brown. Today Bob Brown owns the Amigo Ecology Corporation which manufactures the box. He is also a millionaire.

Scientists and manufacturers are constantly on the lookout for new ways to apply existing things. George Washington Carver thought up over three hundred useful articles in which peanuts could be used. Manufacturers of basic materials and new synthetic materials have to come up with new ways that people can use their products. Rubber, aluminum, cellophane, nylon and Fiberglass are cases in point. The number of applications that have been thought using any one of those basic materials would take volumes to document. Yet every one of them is the result of asking, "What else can we use this for?"

What's Being Wasted That Can Be Put to Use?

Many by-products once considered wasteful have become quite profitable. In Japan, a machine has been designed that turns garbage into construction blocks. The odorfree steel-clad blocks are unbreakable as foundations in boggy areas, as flood-control dikes or as landfill. In the steel industry, slag was once considered a costly waste. Now it's used for making cement, processing building blocks, and some of it is used as a soil conditioner. An old axiom from the meat-packing industry is "We use everything but the squeal." Every part of a processed pig finds its way into some product.

Rejects can sometimes be converted into useful by-products as well. Someone at B. F. Goodrich once saw pieces of surgical tubing being thrown away. He suggested cutting them into rubber bands to hold small items together. For his suggestion he received $150, and Goodrich turned waste into a profitable product.

The "what's being wasted" question may well snatch us all from the jaws of the energy crisis. John Albert, a chemist, has come up with a system for heating buildings with elephant dung and whole-wheat flour. Another ingenious soul, Ben Blumberg, has a scheme to supply everyone in this country with a stationary bicycle attached to a small electric generator. Blumberg calculates that if we all pedal just four hours per day, enough electricity could be generated to save one hundred million barrels of oil each year!

What Else Is Like This?

Asking this question is an application of using analogies to generate new ideas. For example, George Thomas was looking for a better way to apply underarm deodorant. Using the ballpoint pen as his model, he invented the world's first roll-on-deodorant applicator. (Needless to say, the value of this discovery will increase tenfold if Ben Blumberg succeeds in getting us all to pedal four hours each day.)

Using the retractable landing gear of airplanes as a model, Mathew Durda has come up with Pop Wheels, a shoelike device that will get you through an airport faster than O. J. Simpson. If you're walking to a meeting and you realize you're running late, it's no problem when you're wearing Pop Wheels. All you do is lift up each foot, press a button and you're on roller skates. As Durda put it, "It's almost like something out of a James Bond movie. The hinges come up and down like airplane landing wheels. You walk down the street, reach down and pop your wheels, and you're gone. The wheels are small, so it looks like you're floating on air." Asking the question "What else is like this?" causes your mind to search for existing principles and concepts that can be used to solve the problem you're wrestling with.

What Else Can Be Adapted?

The ability to adapt often has spelled the difference between poverty and prosperity. For example, at the World's Fair in 1905, Ernest A. Hamwi was selling a wafer-thin Persian waffle called Zalabia with little or no success. A nearby ice cream stand, in contrast, was overwhelmed with customers and ran out of dishes. Seeing his chance, Hamwi took a hot Zalabia, fashioned it into a cone, let it cool, and served it with a scoop of ice cream on top of it. The delicious dish became known as the "World's Fair Cornucopia" and was a tremendous success.

After the fair, Hamwi founded the Missouri Cone Company and today he is credited as being the father of the ice-cream cone.

Fifteen-year-old Chester Greenwood of Farmington, Maine, was also rather proficient at the art of adaptation. In 1873 Chester received a pair of ice skates for Christmas and rushed down to the local pond to try them out. The fierce cold of the Maine winter was a bit much for Chester and he quickly returned to the house with his ears stinging fiercely. Determined to beat Jack Frost, Chester experimented with several types of earwear until he fashioned the perfect instrument: two pieces of fur attached to an arc of wire. Chester labeled his new invention "Greenwood's Champion Ear Protectors" and had it patented. Chester, his mother and grandmother started producing earmuffs for neighbors, and the demand steadily grew. Eventually, Chester became a millionaire and Farmington became the "Earmuff Capital of the World."

Is There Something I Can Duplicate?

To be in favor of creativity and innovation is like endorsing motherhood. Who could be against it? Yet the fact remains that despite its merit, innovation can be terribly risky. Many large successes have been founded on imitation rather than innovation. IBM got into computers as an imitator. The same holds true for the following:

- General Motors got into autos as an imitator.
- Texas Instruments got into transistors as an imitator.
- Holiday Inns got into motels as an imitator.
- Lytton got into savings and loans as an imitator.
- Playboy got into publishing and entertainment as an imitator.

Japan has built its postwar prosperity by manufacturing and selling products innovated in the United States. It's always an excellent idea to keep your eye out for an idea or product or service you believe you can do better. Ask yourself if there's a style you can emulate or someone's book out of which you can take a leaf. For example, the idea of Book-of-the-Month

Club has been adapted to Hobby-of-the-Month, Candy-of-the-Month and so on. Thomas Edison put it this way: "Make it a habit to keep on the lookout for novel and interesting ideas that others have used successfully. Your idea needs to be original only in its adaptation to the problem you are working on."

How Can This Be Done Better and More Cheaply?

Inflation has most of us suffering from malnutrition of the wallet. Coming up with the right answer to this question can be a literal asset.

Antoine Feuchtwanger provides a classic example of cost cutting coupled with innovation. Feuchtwanger, a Bavarian immigrant, first introduced the frankfurter to America in 1880. Operating from a small stand in St. Louis, Antoine found himself in the midst of an economic quandary. He couldn't afford to serve his franks with standard china and silverware, and the tasty little sausages were too hot for customers to handle with their fingers. At first, Feuchtwanger tried handing out gloves to each customer, but this too proved costly. The laundry bill for the gloves was too high and some people walked off with them. Finally Antoine hit on a great idea. Why not serve it in a long, sliced roll? Today the consumption of hot dogs in the United States is about sixteen billion per year. A little imagineering can go a long way, if you've got a hot product.

How Can This Be Made More Appealing?

This question is best used for ideation by breaking it into the following subquestions: How can we make it look better? Feel better? Sound better? Smell better? Taste better? For example, if the problem is how to make a steak more appealing, such answers might be generated as add parsley, tenderize the meat, serve it sizzling on a metal platter, cook it near or at the dining area and marinate it before cooking.

One ingenious soul used the concept of increased eye appeal to solve the problems created by a garbage strike. Instead of letting the garbage pile up on his front steps, he gift-wrapped it and left it on the front seat of his car with the windows rolled down.

Taking a product and improving its consumer appeal has launched many companies into premier positions of their industry. IBM captured the bulk of the computer market by selling software while others sold hardware. General Motors became the leading automobile manufacturer by being the first to sell autos with different styles, colors and options. Ford insisted on mass-producing one standard, black, unvarying model. As Henry Ford once said, "The customer can have a car in any color as long as it's black." At one time, Ford had two-thirds of the automobile market, but Ford's adherence to rigid mass-production techniques was a very costly policy.

What Can Be Substituted?

Saccharin is a low-calorie substitute for sugar. Solar, nuclear and hydroelectric power are substitutes for petroleum. Automobiles are being made lighter by using parts made from aluminum and plastics instead of steel. Soybean products are sold in stores as high-protein meat substitutes. Innovation and substitution are interwoven in today's world.

One handy substitution made a place for Sylvan Goldman in the history books. In 1937, Goldman, the owner of two supermarket chains, realized that customers were only able to purchase as much as they could carry around the store. This meant that customers usually limited their buying to what they could carry in their arms or a basket. Realizing he had a basket case on his hands, Goldman set out to invent a device that would hold up to $20 worth of groceries (remember, this was 1937). The result of his ingenuity was the invention of the shopping cart, of which there are twenty to twenty-five million in the world today. The only other four-wheeled vehicle that outnumbers it is the automobile.

Mary Phelps Jacob also found her place in history via substitution. In 1914 Jacob was a nineteen-year-old New York debutante who yearned for freedom from the stays and laces of her corset. One Saturday evening before going out she stitched together two lace handkerchiefs and a pink ribbon. Mary had invented the first modern brassiere. She soon realized that her new innovation had tremendous financial potential and had it patented. Mary tried to manufacture and sell the "Backless Brassiere" on her own to no avail. Consequently, she sold the patent to Warner Brothers Corset Company for $15,000. Over the next twenty years Warner Brothers made over twenty million dollars on Mary's bra. Mary was robbed. Why didn't she sue them for nonsupport?

What Should Be Subtracted?

A great deal of creativity consists of adding and combining ideas. However, it's also possible to solve problems and innovate by removing parts or ingredients from an existing idea or thing. For example, did you know that the original American doughnut didn't have a hole? The original had a nut in the center, hence the name *doughnut*. Captain Hanson Crockett Gregory is credited as the "Father of the Doughnut Hole." There are several stories of how the doughnut hole came to be, but the most believable one is that Hanson was watching his mother cook a batch of cakes and noticed that the centers didn't cook thoroughly. He poked a hole in the center of one with a fork, and the doughnut hole was created. What a creation! Quick, simple, practical.

Researchers at Clemson University have come up with a way to breed chickens without feathers. Word has it that the featherless chickens are tastier and consume less feed inasmuch as they don't grow feathers. Only time will tell if this is a real breakthrough in poultry science or just another feather-brained scheme.

By eliminating most of the dimples on a golf ball, two inventors have come up with a golf ball that resists hooking and slicing. The modified ball only has dimples around the equator, and the polar regions of the ball are smooth and have a thicker skin. When an avid duffer strikes the ball on one pole, it develops a life and a gyroscopic spin that keeps it from veering to either side. It's appropriately called the Happy Non Hooker.

Can It Be Done Faster?

In our hurry-up world there's always a need for products and services that can do more in less time. Computers do lightning-fast calculations and print out reams of data at thousands of lines per minute. Airplanes exist that can surpass the speed of sound. Microwave ovens cook in minutes or seconds meals that used to take hours. Our culture is hooked on instant everything, and if you can do it faster, the world is your oyster.

No better example of this exists than that of Clarence Birdseye. The concept of freezing food was not new. Eskimos had been freezing meat, fish and vegetables for ages. What Birdseye invented was a process of fast freezing. He discovered through trial and error that when fresh food was exposed to a circulating mist of brine at minus 45 degrees, the tissues would freeze almost instantly without forming ice crystals. The result of this process is that thawed foods will retain most of their original flavor and texture. In 1922 Birdseye sold his patented process and plant to the Postum Corporation for twenty-two million dollars.

H. L. Mencken, humorist, came up with a novel idea for answering his correspondence faster. Swamped with controversial letters, Mencken devised a reply that made reading them unnecessary. To every letter he tactfully replied: "Dear Sir (or Madam): You may be right."

What Ideas Can Be Combined?

The process of combining ideas to create is called *synthesis*. The fountain pen or ballpoint is the result of combining pen and ink. Alloys are made by combining metals. Ben Franklin got tired of changing from one set of specs to another. Why not combine them? The result was the first pair of bifocals. Thinking up by using combinations is as old as creativity itself.

All of us remember Copernicus as the astronomer who first theorized that the earth travels around the sun rather than vice versa. However, Copernicus also came up with a combination that still exists today. In addition to astronomy, Copernicus was an excellent military commander and medical man. The story goes that a plague broke out among his men and he discovered the cause to be the bread they were eating. The bread was essential to their diet, and Copernicus tried several ways of treating the bread to prevent the spread of disease. One thing he tried was coating the bread with a creamy paste made from churned milk. It didn't cure the plague but it sure tasted good. The practice caught on and rapidly spread throughout sixteenth-century Europe. Thus, in addition to his astronomical achievements, Copernicus was the father of buttered bread.

The ultimate example of combining ideas in literature is the *Reader's Digest*. After World War I, Dewitt Wallace conceived the idea of condensing and combining the best of current reading. The idea was so successful that today *Reader's Digest* sells over thirty million copies in fifteen languages each month.

How Can This Be Condensed?

As a small child I remember reading Dick Tracy in the comics and marveling at his wrist radio. Try and impress today's eight-year-old with a wrist radio and you'll most likely get a yawn from him.

Technology is making things smaller and more compact. The bigger-is-better ethic is on its way out. Nowhere is this more apparent than in the computer field where today's minicomputers can outperform the giant UNIVAC of thirty years ago. Automobiles are rapidly being scaled down, and the gas guzzler will soon be a bit of nostalgia. The energy crisis will also likely reduce the average size of new houses and office buildings. Emphasis will be placed on making more economical use of existing space. Small is in.

Simply looking for a way to make things smaller isn't enough by itself. You must strive for an idea that will shine like a dime among pennies. Transistor radios looked like this next to tube radios when they first appeared. Another example that comes to mind is the folding umbrella.

Leisure Time Development, Inc., has come up with a unique way to apply miniature technology to the problems of dieting. They manufacture a tiny tape-player that fits inside a refrigerator. Each time the door is opened, a voice shouts: "Are you eating again? No wonder you look the way you do. Do yourself a favor and shut the door."

By inventing a miniature electric mixer, Ronald M. Popeil has come up with a device that will scramble an egg while it's still in the shell. The Egg Scrambler sold by Ronco Teleproducts, Inc. (of which Mr. Popeil is chairman) consists of a needle in a cup mounted on a miniature electric motor. To scramble an egg in the shell, you gently impale the egg on the needle, press down until the motor starts, count to five slowly, lift the egg off and break it into the pan. Says Mr. Popeil: "It isn't just another gadget. Not only is there no mess but you get the perfectly blended egg." Maybe if Mr. Popeil teamed up with the Clemson researchers, they could breed a chicken that lays scrambled eggs.

One final anecdote on the value of condensation. A New Orleans firm announced that it would pay twenty-five dollars for any money-saving ideas submitted by employees. The first payment went to the employee who suggested the award be cut to ten dollars.

How Else Can This Be Arranged?

Rearrangement of things and ideas out of their normal order often results in new insights. Additionally, rearrangement offers practically limitless alternatives. A baseball manager can arrange his batting order 362,880 different ways. Try helping someone rearrange the living room furniture and you'll quickly realize how many options there are.

Rearrangement of working times has proved helpful to some businesses. Some companies have adopted the policy of flexitime where individuals are given the option of arranging their schedules. Early birds choose to come in at six and leave at two, whereas late bloomers prefer to come in at ten and leave at six. Provided the nature of the business permits it, flexitime has made everyone happier.

Rearranging methods of rewarding employees is often helpful to organizations. A St. Louis hardware company, trying to reduce employee absenteeism and tardiness, established a unique incentive plan. Employees who came to work on time for a month were eligible for a drawing at the end of the month. One prize was awarded for each twenty-five eligible employees. At the end of six months, employees with perfect attendance could draw for a television set. Absenteeism and tardiness were substantially reduced and sick-leave costs declined 62 percent.

Historian Alistair Cooke was confronted with finding an effective way to arrange books about the various regions of the United States. First he tried alphabetizing them by the author's name and found this ineffective. He had trouble remembering every author's name. Then he tried alphabetizing by state, but this too had problems. Where would he put a book about the Great Plains states or the Mississippi Valley. Finally, he came up with an effective idea. Books about the Great Plains went in the middle of the bookshelf; books about Florida went in the lower right hand corner; books about Texas were placed in the middle of the bottom shelf. He now had a simple system where he could research any region of the United States by scanning the corresponding region of his bookshelf.

In 1873 Joseph Glidden of Dekalb, Illinois, did some interesting rearranging. He stuck some wire into a coffee grinder, turned the handle, and out came a new invention: barbed wire.

What's the Opposite of This?

Vice-versa thinking is a favorite technique of creative people. Just about anything can be reversed, and this contrasting of ideas is a tremendous source of idea fluency. What's the negative of this? Can we turn it upside down? What if we reverse roles? Questions such as these can provide us with a myriad of new ideas! As the old journalism cliché states: "When a dog bites a man it isn't news. But when a man bites a dog, that's news." Some of our greatest breakthroughs have been ideas that were polar opposites of the current beliefs of their day. The ideas of Columbus and Copernicus are cases in point.

A great deal of humor is the result of vice-versa thinking. The movie *Rabbit Test* was about the first male to give birth. One of the funniest skits I remember seeing was about Hell's

Grannys, a motorcycle gang of elderly women who terrorized innocent victims.

The city of Eckley, Pennsylvania, also has capitalized by being an opposite. In 1969 Paramount Pictures chose it as the location for filming *The Molly Maguires*. Paramount wanted a dirty, rundown, gloomy, coal-mining town reminiscent of a century ago. They spent a half-million dollars to make Eckley look ugly and old. TV antennas, stop signs and aluminum awnings were removed. A thick layer of mud was spread over the main street to make Eckley look as it did one hundred years ago. After filming, Paramount offered to return the city to its original look, but the local residents refused. They preferred the old look and decided to open the town to tourists as an authentic 1860 Pennsylvania mining town. Today Eckley proudly calls itself "The Ugliest Town in America."

Another city, Ocean Shores, Washington, annually celebrates "Undiscovery Day" commemorating the night in 1792 when Captain George Vancouver sailed past Ocean Shores *without* discovering it. Every year citizens gather on the beach at midnight and celebrate the moment by yelling, "Hey, George!"

On a more serious note, Dr. Albert Rothenberg has done a great deal of research concerning the use of opposites in the creative process. One special form is what Rothenberg terms "janusian thinking," a thought process named after Janus, the Roman god who was portrayed having two faces, each looking in the opposite direction. As Rothenberg puts it, "In janusian thinking two or more opposites or antitheses are conceived *simultaneously*, either as existing side by side, or as equally operative, valid, or true." After years of research which included collecting data on creative thinking in the work of people such as Einstein, O'Neill, Conrad, Mozart and Picasso, Rothenberg has found that janusian thinking frequently appears at crucial points in the creation and development of their work. However, such thinking seldom appears in the final product. For example, the key to Einstein's development of the general theory of relativity was his hypothesis that a person falling from the roof of a house was both in motion and at rest at the same time. Rothenberg has also found the following examples of janusian thinking: While writing *The Iceman Cometh*, Eugene O'Neill was obsessed by the suicide of a friend. His friend had been troubled over his wife's infidelity, but at the same time he had wanted her to be unfaithful. In conceiving his novel *Nostromo*, Joseph Conrad had the key idea of a criminal who was both good and evil simultaneously. Sketches for Picasso's mural *Guernica* showed a female figure looking into a room and looking out to a courtyard at the same time. James Watson used janusian thinking in discovering the double-helical structure of the DNA molecule. The way you apply janusian thinking is to ask, "What's the opposite of this?" and think of the opposites existing at the same time.

What If Nothing Is Done?

Some of the best discoveries come about from not doing anything and letting nature take its course. Take the case of Cleveland's Clarence Crane. Crane's principal business was chocolate, but he sold hard mints in the summer when chocolate sales declined. He employed a local pill manufacturer to press the mints into shape. The machine malfunctioned and instead of plain round disks they stamped out peppermint rings. Immediately Crane knew he had a unique product and he registered the Life Savers trademark that year. The year was 1912, and since then over twenty-nine billion rolls have been sold.

A Self-Questioning Checklist

The value of a checklist for generating ideas was discussed in Chapter Three. The following is a checklist of questions designed to spur ideation:

Put to other uses? New ways to use as is? Other uses if modified?

Adapt? What else is like this? What other idea does this suggest? Does the past offer a parallel? What could I copy? Whom could I emulate?

Modify? New twist? Change meaning, color, motion, sound, odor, form, shape? Other changes?

Magnify? What to add? More time? Greater frequency? Stronger? Higher? Longer? Thicker? Extra value? Plus ingredient? Duplicate? Multiply? Exaggerate?

Minify? What to subtract? Smaller? Condensed? Miniature? Lower? Shorter? Lighter? Omit? Streamline? Split up? Understate?

Substitute? Who else instead? What else instead? Other ingredient? Other material? Other process? Other power? Other place? Other approach? Other tone of voice?

Rearrange? Interchange components? Other pattern? Other layout? Other sequence? Transpose cause and effect? Change pace? Change schedule?

Reverse? Transpose positive and negative? How about opposites? Turn it backward? Turn it upside down? Reverse roles? Change shoes? Turn tables? Turn other cheek?

Combine? How about a blend, an alloy, an assortment, an ensemble? Combine units? Combine purposes? Combine appeals? Combine ideas?*

Now that you're armed with a battery of questions, go try them out on that problem that you've been wrestling with. Odds are you'll come up with plenty of new ideas and one or more of them may just fill the bill. When it comes to new ideas, ask and you shall think up.

*Alex F. Obsorn, *Applied Imagination*, 3rd rev. ed. (New York: Charles Scribner's Sons, 1963), pp. 286–287.

6

How to Evaluate Ideas

*"There are well-dressed foolish ideas just as there are
well-dressed fools."*

—Nicholas Chamfort

SOME YEARS AGO I read a sign which said "Never begin vast
projects with half-vast ideas." That appears to be very sound
advice when taken at face value. However, it gives rise to an
important question: How do you know when you've got a
good idea? That's an *excellent* question. Here's my answer: I
don't know. And neither does anyone else. Ideas by their very
nature are speculative and subject to the unforeseen whims of
the future and numerous oversights. As Anatole France remarked, "To die for an idea is to place a pretty high price upon
conjecture."

Thus far we have discussed ideas in terms of thinking up
and stressed the importance of suspending judgment and criticism. It's now time to consider the final phase of creative
thinking in which judgment and evaluation are brought into
play. I wish I could honestly tell you that most new ideas are
wonderful and useful. But if I did that would be lying. As
John Arnold put it, "Few ideas are in themselves practical. It
is for the want of active imagination in their application rather
than their means of acquisition that they fail of success. The
creative process does not end with an idea—it only starts with
an idea."

Turning an idea into an innovation means investing your
time, effort and sometimes money into something which may
or may not pay off. There is no way to innovate and avoid
risk, but there are some things you can do to reduce it and
stack the cards more in your favor. In this chapter we will

consider some successfully used guidelines and criteria for judging ideas with the goal of reducing risk. The guidelines won't absolutely tell you which ideas are good but they will weed out many of those that are bad. You may wish to think of the process as one of sifting through the dirt to find the few diamonds.

STRIVE FOR OBJECTIVITY

Whether you use one or some or all of the evaluative criteria, you must above all strive to be objective during this final stage of the creative process. Try to divorce yourself from your ideas and view them from a cool and detached perspective. It isn't easy or entirely possible to do. Total objectivity doesn't exist. However, the more objective you can be about your ideas, the greater the likelihood of ridding yourself of the poor ones.

Get Outside Opinions

Can other people help? Yes, provided they are the right people. At this stage, friends and relatives are rarely useful because they usually lack objectivity as much or more than you. Moreover, they may tell you they love your ideas to spare your feelings when, in truth, they think your schemes are terrible. The fact that Aunt Martha loves your idea for a novel about the cockroach that ate Milwaukee means nothing (unless Aunt Martha happens to be a big publisher). The support of friends and relatives is a wonderful asset but solicit it *after* you've decided that this is an idea worth committing yourself to.

In striving for objectivity, experts can help and often do. However, if the idea involves a significant commitment on your part, it's advisable to get the independent judgment of at least two of them. And be sure to consider their recommendations as recommendations and not as final decrees. Experts make mistakes just like everyone else. Moreover, most of them tend to be extremely well trained in the art of knowing why something can't be done. The narrow specialization of their training leaves many of them nonreceptive to new approaches to problems.

One final recommendation about experts: be sure that they have no personal interest or stake in your ideas which may tend to cloud their objectivity. The first law of expert advice is that you don't ask the barber if you need a haircut.

Sleep on Your Ideas First

A good idea for increasing your objectivity is to let a fair amount of time elapse between thinking up and judging. Sleep on your ideas or put them aside for several days or weeks. Let them cool off. (I assume you've written them down.) This will reduce your emotional attachment, and the passage of time will give you a fresh perspective. An added bonus is that you will likely have some additional ideas since you have given your subconscious more time for incubation. As a writer I find the practice of putting my thoughts on ice to be invaluable. Immediately after writing, I frequently may feel that I've done a very good or poor job. However, sometime the great ideas don't seem so great the next day. And I've also found that some of my best ideas were ones that I initially felt were poor. Never underestimate the perspective of time as an asset for judging ideas.

PRIMARY CRITERIA FOR JUDGING IDEAS

Assuming you have given your ideas time to cool off, the following are guidelines that will aid you in evaluating their worth. These criteria are discussed from the viewpoint that you alone are the sole judge. However, they can also be used by groups who may wish to vote on each idea that's presented. When using team creative techniques some organizations have found it wise to use one group for thinking up and another group for evaluating.

Is It Effective?

Effectiveness means results. Will the idea fill the bill? Will it do the job? Will it work? Is it good enough to make a meaningful contribution? If the idea is one for saving energy, will it actually save energy? Or if it's an idea for saving money, will it really save money? If it's an idea for a safety device, will it make things safe? Most ideas will not pass this first crucial test. Therefore you must be very honest with yourself. If the answer to the effectiveness question is no, don't give up the idea immediately. With further effort you may be able to improve it and come up with something that will be effective. Thomas Edison actually tested over six thousand varieties of material before he came up with an effective filament for the electric light.

Is It Efficient?

Given that an idea is effective, another question arises. Is it a significant improvement over the status quo? Have you come up with an idea where a great deal is to be gained from implementing it, or have you reinvented the wheel? Your idea must be better in some way than the idea it's designed to replace. Otherwise there will be no incentive to adopt it. If you'll pardon the cliché, this criterion asks you if your idea will produce a better mousetrap.

Referring back to the electric light, Dr. Irving Langmuir set out to design and build a better light bulb than the original Edison lamp. He began by first trying to find out why the lamps tended to blacken on the inside. He improved the vacuum in the bulbs, but they still tended to blacken. Then he tried substituting gases for the vacuum and found that argon was the best gas. He then discovered that the bulbs could be improved by just the right coiling of the filament. All of this resulted in a gas-filled lamp that had twice the efficiency of the vacuum tungsten lamp.

Is It Compatible with Human Nature?

The so-called Harvard Law of Animal Behavior says that under the most carefully controlled conditions, organisms behave as they damn well please. This law certainly applies to people. Your idea may be effective, efficient and a tremendous boon to mankind. It may solve a very pressing problem or fill a universal need. But if people have to modify or radically alter their behavior to adopt your idea, its chances for success are slim or nil.

Some years back auto manufacturers learned this lesson the hard way. In 1974 the new models came out with an added safety feature. The engine couldn't be started unless the seatbelts were fastened. Until you buckled up, you weren't going anywhere. Irate owners complained, sales fell off and the manufacturers took quick steps to eliminate this feature. Despite the fact that seatbelts save lives, most people felt buckling up was just too much of a bother.

As a positive example, IBM captured 80 percent of the computer market by making an innovation fit the needs of users. Coupled with excellent marketing, IBM developed software packages that were tailored to help individual customers. They rented and serviced their computers and made them easy for businesses to use. While its competitors stressed building better computers, IBM provided and sold better service. In effect, they tamed the "electronic brain" to make it compatible with the behavior of potential users.

Is It Compatible with Your Goals?

There is no substitute for motivation. The sheer determination of an individual can turn a seemingly mediocre idea into a smashing success. Behind the creation of any great innovation, discovery or organization is at least one individual who was consumed by a driving force to make an idea or a dream succeed. These are the people who take aim at a target and will the arrow into the bull's eye.

The only way you or anyone else can acquire this kind of sustained motivation is from within. In effect, this criterion is asking you, "How badly do you want to try this idea?" Does it go against the grain of what you want out of life? If so, forget it. However, if you find yourself consumed by an idea, take charge and give it all you've got. The more you want to do something, the more you will automatically and willingly give of yourself to the task at hand. This greatly increases your chances of success.

Is the Timing Right?

You don't introduce a new fur coat in April or a new line of bathing suits in October. Remember the Edsel? Part of the reason for this classic debacle was bad timing. It appeared on the market as a luxury car during an economic recession. To make bad matters worse, it came out just after the Soviet Union upstaged the United States by successfully putting the first man-made satellite into orbit. Sputnik and the recession had the American public in a very sober, conservative frame of mind, and the Edsel wasn't a conservative car. Market research indicated a need for a product like the Edsel, but this data had been gathered several years earlier during a period of economic prosperity when people were more inclined and able to spend money on a new, somewhat fancy automobile.

You must consider your ideas from the standpoint of timing and a great deal of this is pure guesswork. Let's face it. If you had a perfect sense of timing, you could make millions each day on Wall Street. In judging the timing of an idea, start first with the present. Would it be practical right now as conditions exist? How long will it take to turn the idea into a reality? What's the future going to be like when it's implemented? Are there any trends developing that will make this idea more or less valuable in the future than today? Would this idea have been more or less valuable in the past than today? Be sure to consider every idea from the standpoint of the time frame in which it will be implemented. There is no such thing as the right idea at the wrong time.

Is It Feasible?

The feasibility criterion asks two questions: 1) Can it be done? and 2) If it can be done, is it worth it? Some ideas may be very effective solutions to problems, but the means to implement them may not be available or even exist. (The energy crisis would end today if someone came up with an engine that could be fueled with water in lieu of gasoline, but unfortunately such technology *does not yet* exist.) It's a great idea but unfeasible. Other ideas can be readily implemented, but the cost in time, effort and money are just too great to justify the benefits. For example, there are millions of tons of gold in the seas and oceans of the world. The technology to extract it exists, but the cost of extracting the metal is more than it's worth. It wouldn't be wise to spend several thousand dollars to make your home more energy efficient if you estimated that it would only save you one hundred dollars per year in fuel bills. The cost-benefit ratio indicates that this is an unfeasible idea.

Is It Simple?

I've already stressed the need for simplicity in light of our tendency to overcomplicate in today's world. Today, simplicity is at a premium due to its scarcity and a valuable criterion for judging ideas. Given two or more relatively equal ideas, choose the simpler one first.

If an idea rates highly on these seven criteria, it's a relatively safe bet that you have a very practical one that's worth pursuing. In addition to these criteria, there are two other checklists of questions for judging ideas. You may find them helpful as I have when assessing the value of a brainchild.

The Value Engineering Principle
1. What is it?
2. What does it do?
3. What does it cost?
4. What else will do the job?
5. What does that cost?

The U.S. Navy Checklist

1. Will it increase production—or improve quality?
2. Is it a more efficient utilization of manpower?
3. Does it improve methods of operation, maintenance or construction?
4. Is it an improvement over the present tools and machinery?
5. Does it improve safety?
6. Does it prevent waste or conserve materials?
7. Does it eliminate unnecessary work?
8. Does it reduce costs?
9. Does it improve present methods?
10. Will it improve working conditions?

The Navy checklist, value engineering principle and the seven criteria may not be applicable to all ideas that you're evaluating. For example, let's assume you're retiring and have the financial means to live anywhere in the United States. You've brainstormed a long list of desirable places to live. Any of the criteria previously listed will provide you with little or no help. You have to develop your own set of guidelines. Thus, you begin generating judgmental factors for evaluating such as cost of living, population, climate, transportation, social and recreational activities, access to medical-care facilities and any other factors that are important to you. Then you can evaluate each potential retirement site in terms of its value in light of the criteria. The point is that in evaluating ideas, you will frequently have to think up your own set of criteria. This will be particularly true for personal problems.

The Idea Evaluation Matrix

No matter what the problem, ideas or criteria are, one very helpful tool in evaluating is the idea evaluation matrix illustrated in Figure 1. You use this tool by listing each of your ideas in the left-hand column and the criteria in the appropriate column headings at the top of the form. Each idea can then be measured in light of each of the criteria. If the idea fares well in light of the criteria, put a G (for *good*) in the appropriate box. If it's fair, put an F and P (for *poor*) if the idea doesn't measure up. Spaces are also provided to check off if the idea is to be used, held for further consideration, or rejected. Finally, on the right-hand side is a space for any additional thoughts for modifying ideas that will improve their effectiveness in light of the criteria. The value of using the matrix is that it forces you to organize your thoughts when judging ideas. When you're able to see how each idea measures up alongside the others, it increases the odds of choosing the better ones.

Testing Your Ideas

Let's assume you've come up with a great idea. It measures up beautifully against every yardstick you can think of. Should you proceed full speed with total commitment? My recommendation is that you do this only if you feel it's the only alternative. One final way to evaluate ideas is to test them out on a small scale. Aircraft manufacturers build models of airplanes and test them in wind tunnels before risking the life of a test pilot. Companies frequently test-market a new product or service in one or a few towns before pouring large sums of money into a nationwide marketing effort. Before writing this book, I constructed an outline and submitted it to the publisher, who agreed it was a worthwhile idea and offered a contract. This spared me the risk of writing an entire book and not having it published. The point is that you can frequently test out your ideas on a small scale before plunging head-first into a gigantic commitment. If your idea involves a considerable commitment, testing it out on a small scale or for a short period of time is another worthwhile risk-reducing technique.

Certainly, idea testing isn't foolproof. Test pilots have been killed trying out new airplanes. Just because the product sells in Indianapolis doesn't ensure that it will sell in Houston, Los Angeles or New York. Every book publisher enthusiastically signs up a new book idea fully aware that only one book in three will turn a profit. Testing is just one more thing to consider as a possible final step in evaluating.

Not all ideas can be tested. Decisions such as selling the

house or quitting your present job are usually irrevocable, and these are choices that will really test your courage. In such a case, gather the best information you can (realizing that you'll never have enough), make a decision in light of the criteria and get on with the business of living. No good can come from looking back and second-guessing your decisions. Everyone has 20–20 hindsight.

PRESENTING YOUR IDEAS

The fact that you're sold on a new idea is only the beginning. Getting it off the ground and moving it toward an innovative reality frequently starts with selling your idea to others. The following guidelines are presented to help you design an effective way of convincing others of the value of your ideas.

1. Be sure that you have thought through the idea completely and that it is clear in your own mind. If your ideas are cloudy, vague or poorly thought out, discussing them with others will only lessen the chances of their adoption. Hold off on discussing or presenting your ideas until they're crystal clear to you. The time to present your idea to others is *after* you have thought it through.

2. Choose a proper time, place and media. If it's an oral presentation you're making, try to present it at a time and place where you feel the audience is most likely to be receptive. Consider using photographs, charts, models, illustrations or anything you can think of that will help you present your idea in a favorable light.

3. Organize and develop your presentation around a need or needs. Presumably your idea is worthy because it provides a necessary service. Decide what it is and make the filling of this need the main point of your presentation. Be sure that your presentation is well organized and that your audience understands how it is organized. This will make it easier for them to understand the points you're trying to make.

4. Describe how you came up with the idea and why it's better than what presently exists. This also will enable people to better understand and grasp your point of view. You can

Figure 1   Idea Evaluation Matrix

SOURCE: Ruth B. Noller, Sidney J. Parnes, Angelo M. Biondi, *Creative Actionbook*, rev. ed. of *Creative Behavior Workbook* (New York: Charles Scribner's Sons, 1976), p. 72.

also help your case by demonstrating how you evaluated your idea and what criteria you used. This will convince your audience that you've thought this through and it isn't just a hare-brained scheme you threw together.

5. Don't oversell your idea. Benjamin Franklin gave the following advice: "The way to sell an idea to another is to state your case moderately and accurately. This causes your listener to be receptive and, like as not, he will turn about and convince you of the worth of your idea. But if you go at him in a tone of positiveness and arrogance, you are likely to turn him against your idea, no matter how good it is." When you state your case moderately, accurately and intelligently, you're in effect paying your audience a compliment. You're telling him, "I think that you're a reasonable, intelligent and open-minded person who can readily understand the value of my idea without being clubbed over the head with it." Respect breeds respect, and likely as not he will respond with respect for your idea.

6. Summarize the key points of your presentation at the end. Be sure to reiterate the need that your idea fills and express any enthusiasm, optimism or passion that you feel for the idea. Enthusiasm is contagious, and if you can demonstrate it in an unarrogant way, it will likely spread to some or all of the audience.

Evaluating ideas is the final and a terribly crucial step in the idea-generating process. It involves separating the wheat from the chaff, and there aren't any surefire methods that will work all the time. The most you can hope for is to reduce the odds of picking a loser, and the guidelines presented in this chapter will aid you to that end.

PART III

CLEARING THE HURDLES BETWEEN IMAGINATION AND REALIZATION

7

Imagineers Need
Peace of Mind

"For peace of mind, resign as general manager of the universe."

—Larry Eisenberg

CREATIVE SUCCESS DEPENDS heavily on peace of mind and a positive mental attitude. The person with a healthy self-respect and who feels in charge of himself is the one most able to focus his mind in the relaxed manner that is so crucial to generating new ideas. The idea that the most creative people are highly frustrated, suffering and under a great deal of negative stress is simply a myth. It's possible to be creative under stress, but the new ideas come in spite of and not because of it.

In today's fast-paced, urban life-style, peace of mind is at a premium. Norman Vincent Peale observed, "America has become so tense and nervous it has been years since I've seen anyone asleep in church—and that is a sad situation." Do any of the following incidents sound like you? You worked late one night on a pet project and the boss chewed you out the next morning for being late. You were late because your car gave up the ghost on the freeway. Your growing family needs a bigger house but you're struggling to make the payments on the one you have. Two of your children are nearing college age and a third one needs braces. Your salary is coming in a poor second in a race against the cost of living. Everything is going up, including your blood pressure and the acid content of your stomach. Ringing in your ears is the voice of Karl Malden, "What will you do, what *will* you do."

If you're like most of us, you'll try watching television for a few hours as a means to temporarily escape from your problems. What you often find there is anything but peace of mind. Newscasts are filled with accounts of wars, murders, rapes, robberies, strikes, economic pessimism and numerous other tales of disaster and destruction. Daytime television is filled with dramas that act out the dark side of human relationships. Evening programing is sprinkled with a healthy dose of violent drama. Indeed, research on television viewers has shown that most viewers experience a faster heartbeat, more perspiration and a jumpy feeling caused by increased adrenaline flow while watching their favorite programs.

Others of us try mind-altering approaches to peace of mind. Today, drug abuse and alcoholism abound in epidemic proportions. Those who take psychological refuge in drugs or alcohol are confusing peace of mind with absence of mind. To try and create peace of mind with drugs or alcohol is much like trying to heal a broken arm with injections of novocaine.

Lest you think I'm a radical moralist advocating the end of television and a return to Prohibition, let me assure you that I'm not. However, to develop the proper attitudes for creative success we have to understand our feelings, thoughts and any preconceived notions that we may be harboring about them. The more you understand about negative stresses that hinder creative thought and action, the better equipped you'll be to prevent these internal forces from clogging your creative machinery and standing between you and your goals.

WHAT IS THIS STUFF CALLED STRESS?

In a nutshell, stress is anything that makes you feel pressured, tense, on edge or uptight. A certain amount of positive stress is necessary to keep us feeling healthy, active, creative and useful. When you put deadlines on your goals, you create a certain amount of stress that helps you to produce new ideas and things. If you're interviewing for an important job or getting ready to take an important test, a little stress will keep you alert and enable you to perform at your best. All of us feel stress every day, and to cease to feel stress is to cease to live. It's as intertwined with life as sleeping and breathing. It's only when stress begins to inhibit our creativity, health and general feeling of well-being that it becomes a problem.

Inasmuch as all of us are different, what one person finds stressful may not be stressful to another. However, there is a stress-prone personality. These are the people who are always in a hurry, who have to be the best at *everything*, who can't say no to taking on numerous responsibilities and who spread themselves thin in terms of time. Relaxation is difficult for the stress prone. It makes them feel guilty. Consequently, hobbies and diversions from work are few. Stress-prone people push themselves beyond rational limits, and the achievement of exterior goals becomes all important. Personal values take a back seat. To the stress-prone college student, good grades are paramount and learning is secondary. To the stress-prone employee, moving up the corporate ladder quickly takes precedence over the personal fulfillment of doing a job well. Not surprisingly, a ten-year study of business executives found that those who were stress prone were three times more likely to get heart attacks than their less keyed-up counterparts.

Do you believe . . .

1. your feelings and emotions are a mysterious, uncontrollable phenomenon that have you at their mercy?

2. a conscientious, good person is one who worries about the future?

3. feeling bad about what's already happened is fitting punishment for a mistake you've made?

4. your worth as a human being is determined by what other people think of you and what you do?

5. you're responsible for the happiness of other people and they're responsible for yours?

6. living the good life consists of experiencing a never-ending sequence of uncontrollable highly emotional peaks and valleys?

At the deepest level, it's likely that you believe most or all of those statements. These are common societal values that you have been taught by word or deed since you were old enough to understand. The fact is that none of them are inherently true and all of them contribute to the creation of unnecessary negative stress. Most stress is learned behavior.

The important thing about learned behavior is that what is

learned can be unlearned. It isn't easy to eliminate years of habitual conditioning, but the fact is that by getting in touch with your feelings and understanding how they operate, you can begin to program yourself to make your feelings work for rather than against you.

All of us live at the feelings level, and our feelings are in large part a result of the way we perceive things. You observe or are told something, you interpret it, and only then do you have a reaction at the feelings level.

The point is that feeling is preceded by perception, and all of us are capable of controlling our interpretation of what we see. If we can control our interpretation, then it logically follows that we can exercise some control over our feelings as well.

Only You Are in Charge

Blaming others for any stress we feel is very common. It's also a mistake. In the final analysis, you're the only one capable of making yourself feel guilty, sad, enthusiastic or whatever. Your thoughts and feelings are strictly yours and it's the same for all of us. How many times have you heard statements such as "I can't think straight because you upset me" or "You hurt my feelings" or "You make me happy"? Those statements are false because of their impossibility. No one is capable of making you feel a certain way unless you choose to react in that particular manner. More accurate statements would be: "I have chosen to think illogically as a reaction to your behavior," "I choose to feel hurt after hearing what you said" or "I've decided to be happy because of you."

Assuming the responsibility for your own feelings is the first and a giant step toward preventing stress from standing between you and your creative abilities. In the final analysis, the peace of mind and positive attitudes necessary for creative effort won't be determined by what you do or what you have, but rather by what you think. Without further delay, let's take a look at some of the demons that can jam your creative machinery.

Worry—Destructive Imagination

About worry, Walter Kelly wrote, "When I don't have anything to worry about, I begin to worry about that." Are you
one who spends a lot of time worrying? If so, I have good
news. Worries are fantasies about all the horrid things that the
future may bring. If you're a regular worrier, it proves that
you have a very active imagination and have been exercising it
for years. Congratulations! The bad news is that you're using
the gift to hurt rather than help yourself. The fact is that well
over 90 percent of everything we worry about never comes to
pass and the few things that do eventually occur will not be
prevented by worrying. As Evan Esar quipped, "Worry is like
a rocking chair: it gives you something to do but it doesn't get
you anywhere."

Unfortunately, many of us confuse worry with concern and
responsibility. When you tell chronic worriers about the
futility of worrying, their general response is, "Well, somebody has to worry about this. What if everyone were like you
and didn't worry? Things would soon go to hell in a basket."
Goals, action and concern for the future are positive things,
but worry is an unnecessary emotion that prevents us from
enjoying present moments, which is in reality all we have. It
serves absolutely no useful purpose.

Why is worry so popular? There are several reasons for this
universal waste of time and energy. First, we have been taught
that worry is the mark of a caring, concerned, conscientious
soul. Worriers are perceived as responsible people who aren't
enjoying today so that we can all enjoy a better tomorrow.

The truth of the matter is that spending time worrying is a
cop-out for not spending present moments effectively and en-
joyably. If you're busy worrying, you now have an excuse for
not taking constructive action on any problems on the horizon.
Procrastinators are usually great worriers. Furthermore, if you
really get to be an expert worrier, it's possible to make yourself physically ill. And this gives you an excuse for not taking
creative or constructive action in the future. You can just keep
on worrying without changing and enjoy wallowing in self-
pity. You create yourself a blueprint for an uncreative, wasted
life.

Guilt—the Great Manipulator

Similar to worry is another stressful and useless emotion—guilt. The difference between them is one of time. Whereas the worrier feels bad about the future, those consumed by guilt feel bad about the past. They indulge themselves in the luxury of being seduced by what's over and can't be changed. Obviously, it's a complete and total waste to spend present moments feeling remorseful and regretful about yesterday. History is history and nothing can change it. Yet guilt rivals worry as a popular alternative to spending time destructively. Why?

One reason guilt is so prevalent in our lives is that it's society's universal regulatory mechanism. From the cradle to the grave and from the bedroom to the boardroom our lives are governed by guilt. The guilt game is simple. If you don't follow the rules, you pay a penalty by feeling bad about mistakes made in the past. Guilt isn't to be confused with learning from your mistakes and resolving to improve, which is rational and constructive behavior. Instead, guilt wielding has a somewhat vengeful and neurotic quality.

We learn the guilt game early in life from our parents. "I went through nine months of agony to bring you into the world and you embarrass me this way." The implication here is that children are responsible for their parents' feelings. And being very perceptive, children begin using guilt to manipulate parents. "If you really loved me, you'd buy me that ten-speed bike." But that's just the beginning. As we grow up we discover...

1. Teachers use guilt. "Someone as smart as you shouldn't have made a C on that test." The implication here is that you should feel bad about failing to live up to someone else's expectations.

2. Religions use guilt. "You missed church last week which made God sad." (And now you should feel sad.)

3. Bosses use guilt. "We wouldn't have lost that deal if everyone had worked harder."

4. Lovers use guilt. "I wouldn't be so cold if you were different. Even eggs take three minutes."

5. Salesmen use guilt. "Your family deserves the best" or "If something happens to you, your spouse won't be able to pay off the mortgage and send the children to college without this policy." The implication is that you should buy the product or face the consequence of feeling guilty for letting your loved ones down.

Like worry, guilt is a present-moment activity with similar psychological payoffs. As long as you're feeling guilty you don't have to innovate or make the effort to turn new ideas into successful realities. Guilt also lets you take the easy way out by shifting the blame for everything to others. You return to a childlike attitude which abdicates complete control of your life to others and relieves you of the burden of improving and changing yourself. You spend your time feeling guilty and transferring those feelings to others by pointing out their inadequacies. All of which adds up to a sum total of zero achievement and innovation.

Fear

As a destructive stress producer, fear is like worry in that it's usually more the result of imagination than reality. If you doubt this, consider the following survey of over three thousand Americans. They were asked "What are you most afraid of?" The somewhat surprising answers were as follows:

Biggest Fear	Percent Naming
1. Speaking before a group	41
2. Heights	32
3. Insects and bugs	22
3. Financial problems	22
3. Deep water	22
6. Sickness	19
6. Death	19
8. Flying	18

More good creative ability is wasted due to fear than anything else I can think of. People with good voices are afraid to sing. People with artistic talent hide their paintings rather than risk ridicule. People who love to write are too embarrassed to show their writing to anyone.

Why do we take refuge in the darkness of fear rather than step into the light? One reason is because it's easier. It's easier to underestimate our efforts than those of others. It's easier to do nothing than to do something. It's easier to criticize than it is to create. It's easier to sit back and regret missed opportunities than it is to pounce on them. And finally, it's easier to watch the world go by and waste your life than it is to think up and make things happen. It's also no fun.

Anger

A certain amount of anger can be a positive force to motivate creative effort and follow-through, providing it's constructively channeled. However, raging anger will only result in nothing that's of any use to anybody.

Like fear, guilt and worry, anger has neurotic payoffs. The angry person demands that the world live up to his expectations, which is an impossibility. When the world doesn't meet his expectations, he indulges himself by blaming the world and other people. This gets him off the hook and he doesn't have to change or be introspective. He just gives himself license to become incompetent or go temporarily insane. "I have a terrible temper, you know." And all of this rage blocks any possible chance of thinking creatively or constructively. Unfortunately, most new ideas born in anger are destructive.

Perfectionism

Do you strive to be perfect in practically everything you do? If so, you're making a big mistake by reaching for the impossible dream. Furthermore, you're constructing a giant creative hurdle for yourself, for the only way to avoid mistakes is to not do anything. As Winston Churchill remarked, "The maxim 'nothing avails but perfection' may be spelled PARALYSIS."

In order for something to be perfect, there must be a standard of comparison. However, new ideas and things by their very nature can't be measured in terms of perfection. Moreover, standards, no matter what their nature, are usually nothing more than a reflection of someone's opinion. If you come up with a new idea or innovation, it's absurd to think of it in terms of perfection.

Look around you and you'll quickly realize that many of us are harboring some real perfectionistic values. It's no wonder. The educational system teaches us to think this way. The best grades and honors are typically given to the person who makes the least mistakes and not to those students who display originality. This type of thinking carries over into our adult life, and many organizations reward and promote those who do little or nothing wrong. Following orders, procedures and not rocking the boat are rewarded more frequently than running the risk of trying new things. To be human is to make mistakes. Just remember, your actions will be perfect when you're dead.

Habit

Inasmuch as we are all creatures of habit, it's all too easy to fall into the trap of living in a rut. Obviously, there are advantages to forming certain habitual patterns of behavior. However, habit can be carried to a neurotic extreme and cripple your innovative abilities. Are you one who always . . .

- eats the same kind of food?
- drives the same way to work?

- spends your leisure time on the same activities?
- performs your job tasks in the same manner and at the same time?
- wears the same type of clothes?
- associates with the same kind of people?
- discusses the same topics in your conversations with others?

If you answered yes to most or all of those questions, you must be suffering from terminal boredom. Living in a rut creates a false sense of security, which is why many of us opt for this type of behavior. Associating with those who think just like you and doing your job in the exact same way reduces the possibility of coining up with new, more valuable and better ideas which may appear threatening. By surrounding yourself with the familiar, you can feel that you're doing the "right and mature" thing. The reality is you're just doing the same thing and letting the opportunity to live a fulfilling and creative life pass you by.

A Weak Self-image

The greatest single determinant of what you will be or do with your creative abilities is your perception of who you are. Self-esteem is central to the whole problem of securing any type of success in any endeavor. No one is capable of reaching beyond the limits of his own self-imposed boundaries. When you see someone of modest ability experiencing large successes, take a closer look. What you'll find is that while others may have a modest opinion of this person's abilities, he doesn't.

Unfortunately, most of us have been taught to sell ourselves short. We don't start out that way. Small children find it only natural to think highly of themselves. Yet as we mature we are taught that such behavior is selfish and conceited. Remember the mayhem that erupted when Muhammad Ali told the world, "I am the greatest?" People were outraged at such immodesty. Yet the fact is that during his career as a boxer, Ali was indeed the greatest. No doubt, his undying faith in his own abilities was a major contribution to his success.

One of my favorite illustrations about the value of self-esteem is this allegory by William W. Purkey:

> . . . a mouse ran into the office of the Educational Testing Service and accidentally triggered a delicate point in the apparatus just as the College Entrance Examination Board's data on one Henry Carson was being scored.
>
> Henry was an average high-school student who was unsure of himself and his abilities. Had it not been for the mouse, Henry's score would have been average or less, but the mouse changed all that, for the scores that emerged from the computer were amazing—800's in both the verbal and quantitative areas.
>
> When the scores reached Henry's school, the word of his giftedness spread like wildfire. Teachers began to re-evaluate their gross underestimation of this fine lad, counselors trembled at the thought of neglecting such talent, and even college admissions officers began to recruit Henry for their schools.
>
> New worlds opened for Henry, and as they opened he started to grow as a person and as a student. Once he became aware of his potentialities and began to be treated differently by the significant people in his life, a form of self-fulfilling prophecy took place. Henry began to put his mind in the way of great things . . . Henry became one of the best men of his generation.[*]

Our main contact with reality is our concept of who we are, and the fear of losing touch with reality is a very traumatic one. Therefore, for better or worse, all of us have a tendency to cling to beliefs about what strengths and weaknesses we possess. The result is a self-fulfilling prophecy where our beliefs about what we can do determine what we actually can do. If you believe that you lack creative talent and ingenuity, your beliefs will keep the lid on any positive use of your abilities.

---

[*]William W. Purkey, *Self Concept and School Achievement* (Englewood Cliffs, N.J.: Prentice-Hall, 1970), pp. 1–2.

STRATEGIES FOR CLEARING THE PERSONAL HURDLES

Any one of the problems just discussed is capable of shutting down your creative abilities. However, the main point to remember is that these stresses and irrational types of behavior can be controlled by you and will stand between you and creative success only if you allow them to. Personal hurdles are the most difficult to overcome but they're also the most crucial. Without further delay let's look at some things you can do to release the brakes on your creative powers. First we will consider some general techniques and then follow up with specific ideas for specific problems.

Some General Strategies

1. Take a positive approach to your problems. Problems are symptomatic of the fact that you're a living, breathing human being. The only people who have few or no problems are the people who don't have or do anything. Remember that every problem presents an opportunity. Look for that opportunity, and resolve to make the most of it. Such an approach will keep you feeling overwhelmed. Ann Landers has a philosophy I like: "When life hands you a lemon, make lemonade."

I once heard an amusing anecdote that illustrates this point. The story goes that there were twin boys who were identical with one exception. One was an optimist and the other a pessimist. A psychologist decided to conduct an experiment with them and place the boys in a room with a large pile of horse manure. The pessimistic twin sat in the corner and lamented over his fate while the optimist enthusiastically dug into the pile. When asked why he was digging so fiercely the boy replied, "With all this manure, there has to be a pony nearby!" How about you? Are you just sitting there or are you in there digging?

2. Make a conscious attempt to be relaxed. Most of us believe that our feelings determine our behavior, but the reverse is also true. Our behavior can determine our state of

mind. Making a conscious attempt to physically relax can bring about the relaxed mental state so essential for creative thought. When you feel terribly tense and hassled try this:

Assume a comfortable position sitting or reclining. Loosen any tight clothing.

Close your eyes and imagine yourself being in the most tranquil place you can think of. Maybe it's a calm lake or a stream with a picturesque mountain view. Feel the pleasant warmth of the sunlight on your face as you visualize this scene of total tranquillity. Empty your mind of all other thoughts.

Slowly let each part of your body go limp. Breathe deeply and concentrate on relaxing first your forehead and then your chin, neck, arms, torso and legs, in that order. Think of your body as a balloon with the air escaping from it and falling completely depleted.

Remain in this totally relaxed state for ten minutes, or longer if you prefer. Remember that the keys to this exercise are a total physical relaxation and emptying the mind of all thoughts and problems. It's important to have an imaginary retreat where you can relax. Harry Truman used this technique successfully and referred to it as "a foxhole in my mind where I allow nothing to bother me."

3. Meditation techniques can also be very useful. In his book *TM and Business*, Jay Marcus recounts some fascinating stories of people who have used transcendental meditation techniques to bring about creative thought. Such techniques allow our subconscious the opportunity to work by providing the period of incubation that is necessary for illumination. One of the most interesting testimonials came from Doug Henning, who is believed by many to be the greatest magician in the world:

I have had an incredible, absolutely phenomenal increase in my creativity ever since I started meditating in 1974. Before meditating I was using illusions other people invented, even though I was doing them in a different way. After a couple of years of meditating, I began having visions of new illusions, new tricks, during my meditation. I completely redesigned my acts and now even the other magicians don't know how a lot of the things I do are done.

On my last TV special on NBC last December, I actually saw all the illusions in my meditations that I used on the show. I saw them in their finished forms and they came out exactly that way in the show.

A friend suggested TM to me during a particularly difficult time when a show I was involved in was doing poorly. I was worried constantly and the worry kept me from sleeping. I was exhausted. I started TM and suddenly I stopped worrying and started sleeping and the show started to shape up and went on to become a great success.*

Other testimonials from such diverse people as executives, secretaries, physicians and television personalities report that meditation increases their peace of mind, reduces stress and provides them with the psychological climate necessary for creative thought and action. The stories these people tell are convincing and sincere. Perhaps this is a technique that can work for you as well.

4. Always keep your perspective and sense of humor close at hand. Most stress is caused by people who overestimate the importance of their problems. Things are almost always less important than they appear to be in the present. Why treat everything in life as a major catastrophe? Few things actually are. Back off and look at things in a lifetime perspective. As you attempt to innovate, make a conscious effort to enjoy the present. It's all you have. A relaxed and casual approach will enhance your creative effectiveness and improve your sense of well-being. Enjoy, be you and don't take yourself so seriously. As Habib Bourguiba put it, "Happy is the person who can laugh at himself. He will never cease to be amused."

5. Do something for someone else. Continually sitting around and dwelling on your problems is one sure way to create negative stress, and much stress is caused by this. The cure for overconcern with self is simple. Concern yourself with other things and other people. The world needs kindness today more than anything else. Why not provide it? It usually costs little or nothing. A well-placed smile, an encouraging word or a sincere compliment can mean a great deal to some-

*Jay B. Marcus, *TM and Business* (New York: McGraw-Hill, 1977), p. 60.

one else. If someone needs help, ask yourself, "What can I give this person that will help them to help himself?" To the degree that you involve yourself with things outside yourself, you will lessen the odds of being hindered by negative stresses. Both you and the world will be better for it.

Get in Touch with Your Creative Self

One necessary step to unlocking your creative and innovative powers is to view yourself as a creative person. As I pointed out in Chapter One, most of us have been conditioned to think of ourselves as uncreative. Until this hurdle is cleared, little can come from your creative efforts. You simply have to believe in your own creative abilities before you can begin to reap meaningful benefits from them. With that thought in mind, here are some things you can do to strengthen your creative self-image:

1. Set yourself some creative goals, complete with deadlines and a concrete set of plans for achieving them. The best way to think of yourself as innovative is to attempt to become innovative. Start with small tasks. Write that short story, song or enter that advertising-jingle contest. Try to brainstorm as many ideas as you can think of for solving a problem that's plaguing you around the house or at work. Go back and try doing some of the creativity exercises in Chapter Three. The more you actively force yourself to generate ideas, the more ideas you will generate. And as you see the ideas pouring forth, you will gain a greater confidence in your creative abilities.

2. Don't let other people define your creative potential. No one, including you, knows what you're capable of doing or thinking up. Human potential is one of the great imponderables and man is just beginning to wake up to the powers of his own mind. Imagine what would happen if you could go back in time two hundred years and tell American Colonists about all the innovations and technical breakthroughs that would be taking place in the next centuries. They would probably lock you in a dungeon and declare you insane, heretical, sacrilegious or whatever. Few of them would have had the

vision to realize what was possible. There are only two sure things about anybody's creative ability: 1) It's unknown and 2) It's underestimated. Remember that the assumptions you make about your creative power will determine to what extent you develop this most valuable resource. No one knows what you're capable of. So if someone tries to tell you, don't listen. If it seems right and you want to try something, proceed at full speed.

3. Put your own needs first and see to it that they're well satisfied. In his well-known hierarchy of human needs, Abraham Maslow pointed out that the need to be creative will motivate people only when lower and more basic needs are relatively well satisfied. For most of us, this means that we must feel comfortable, secure, socially accepted and have a general feeling of high self-esteem before we are strongly motivated to fulfill our creative potential.

Unfortunately, much of what we are taught prevents this from occurring. Too much of what we learn in the process of growing up centers around sacrificing our own needs for the benefit of others. This usually breeds hostility on the part of all concerned. Until you have a feeling of relative comfort and a healthy level of need satisfactions, anything you can give to others will be small. Human beings have an innate need to give and share with others. However, we give our best out of abundance and our worst out of self-denial. Only when you feel good and self-satisfied with your own life will you be most able to help others with their lives. And your creative abilities will thrive best in an atmosphere of abundance rather than one of deprivation. It's important to be hungry for creative success, but deprivation only prevents you from focusing your energies on being creative. No doubt, there are starving artists, but the same artist can do much better work on a full stomach.

4. Realize that creative ability and creative behavior are two separate things. Just because you haven't utilized your creativity doesn't mean it isn't there. Refuse to believe the ridiculous idea that you aren't creative because you can't recall anything you've done that was creative. You probably use your creative talents in many small ways every day but are unaware of it.

5. Keep a creativity log. Every time you think up a new

idea or project and carry it through, write it down in a special place. Soon you'll begin seeing how much you're using your idea-generating powers, and this in turn will help strengthen your creative self-image.

Replace Guilt, Worry and Fear with Creative Action

Your past is the one part of your life over which you have absolutely no control. No amount of remorse, regret or bad feeling will change history. You do, however, have control over your present and future. If you choose to feel bad about water under the bridge, you're denying yourself the opportunity to enjoy the present and spend your time building a better future.

Let's face it. Reality can be the pits. However, your decision to live a happy and creative life in the present isn't necessarily dependent upon what's happened in the past and what may happen in the future. All you really have are present moments. Get busy and use them creatively. If you spend your time pursuing ideas and goals that are really meaningful to you, you'll become so pleasantly occupied that the ghosts of guilt and worry will fade from your life. Your past will make you miserable only if you allow it to. Positive, creative action today will make for a much happier present and future.

Similarly, the action approach to fear is the best way to conquer it. When fear stands between you and what you want, confront it head on. Ask yourself, "What's the worst that can come from this?" and "Why am I afraid of this?" Being able to verbalize your fears will help make you aware of their irrationality and frequently makes them disappear. Then replace fear with action and plow ahead with gusto. There's a lot of truth to Franklin Roosevelt's "We have nothing to fear but fear itself." As Logan Pearsall Smith put it, "What is more mortifying than to feel you have missed the plum for want of courage to shake the tree?" When fear knocks on the door and courage answers it, there's nobody there.

Vent Your Anger Constructively

1. Realize that you don't have to get angry. We live in an angry society filled with neurotic people who frequently become enraged when things don't go their way. However, this doesn't mean that you have to behave in such a manner. Anger is a conscious reaction to being frustrated and you don't have to become angry when frustrated. Realizing this fact will start you on the road to reducing your anger.

2. Assuming you do get steamed, don't suppress your anger. There are constructive alternatives to venting it. Some people work out their hostilities with regular exercise. Try running, or why not get yourself a punching bag? Or why not learn to play the drums?

3. Try delaying your anger until you can unload it in an undestructive manner. Count to ten or tell yourself that you'll get mad about this tomorrow. And by tomorrow, it may not matter. As Ralph Waldo Emerson wrote, "Grow angry slowly —there's plenty of time."

4. Use your anger to spur you on to creative achievement. Heaven only knows how many great creative works have been born out of someone thinking, "I refuse to be beaten by this" or "I'll show them!" Certainly, anger isn't the best motivator for creative effort. But assuming that you're burdened with it, channel your anger toward positive ends.

5. Rid yourself of the ridiculous notion that you have to get mad in order to be creative. Many people believe this. However, there are much healthier alternatives. Positive and enthusiastic emotions make for better idea production and will create rather than drain energy.

Open Your Mind to New Alternatives

An anonymous philosopher once wrote: "Behold the turtle. He makes progress only when his neck is out." New ideas rarely come from thinking and doing the same old things. Make a conscious effort to introduce change into your life. I'm not arbitrarily suggesting radical, wholesale changes, although sometimes they can be very beneficial. Take stock of everything in your life and question its existence. Ask yourself, "Am I doing this because it's enjoyable and stimulating, or because it's safe?" Make an effort to meet people with varying viewpoints and hear them out. Take up a totally new hobby or pastime. Try visiting or living in another city or country. Replacing the familiar with the unfamiliar is a worthwhile investment in your own growth. In addition to becoming more creative, you'll develop the inner security and self-confidence that can only come from successfully meeting new ideas, people, and situations. Don't allow the security blanket of the familiar to smother your success. If you're ever tempted to do this, remember these words from Evan Esar: "The meek shall inherit the earth—that's the only way they'll ever get it."

If Nothing Is Perfect, Why Should You Be?

The worst mistake you can make is to become overly concerned with making mistakes. Creative success is like war in one respect. If your overall strategy is sound, it's possible to make numerous blunders along the way and still come out on top. However, if your overall strategy is poor, error-free behavior on your part will contribute little to your already poor chances of success. Worse yet, the fear of mistakes can seriously cripple your progress. Don't let this happen.

1. Realize that there is a difference between excellence and perfection and strive for excellence in the things that are most important to you. Excellence is attainable, healthy and rewarding. Perfection is impossible, frustrating and neurotic.

2. Don't fall into the trap of thinking that you have to be good or even moderately successful at everything you do. Al McGuire, a highly successful basketball coach, once remarked: "Winning is overemphasized. The only time it is really important is in surgery and war." If you're having fun there is nothing wrong with painting a mediocre painting or writing a poor short story. Forget about the mistakes and absorb yourself in creating something new. Such a practice actually increases the odds of creative success.

3. Deal with your mistakes rationally. All of us stumble through life making mistakes. It's part of the cost of being

alive. However, every mistake carries a message with it that can help move you closer to achieving your goals. Look for those messages and resolve to learn from them.

4. Accept yourself. St. Francis de Sales wrote, "Have patience with all things, but first with yourself." Never confuse your mistakes with your value as a human being. You're a perfectly valuable, creative, worthwhile person simply because you exist. And no amount of triumphs or tribulations can ever change that. Unconditional self-acceptance is the core of a peaceful mind. And with a peaceful mind, you will have cleared the greatest creative hurdle.

8

Getting People
Behind Your Ideas

*"The inquiring reporter asked the young woman why
she wanted to be a mortician. 'Because,' she said, 'I
enjoy working with people.'*

—San Francisco Chronicle

TURNING IDEAS INTO realities generally involves four major
thrusts:

1. Dealing successfully with people
2. Conquering difficult obstacles
3. Successfully managing your time
4. Creating the enthusiasm and motivation to follow through.

This chapter is about people, and in the succeeding three
chapters we will discuss the other three areas.

SOME COMMON HUMAN OBSTACLES

According to Clark's Law of Revolutionary Ideas, every new
idea, be it in science, politics, art or any other field, evokes
three stages of reaction:

1. "It's impossible. Don't waste my time."
2. "It's possible, but it's not worth doing."
3. "I said it was a good idea all along."

Those three stages summarize what can best be described
as the people hurdle. If you've ever taken on the job of getting
a major, new idea implemented through others, I don't have to
tell you how difficult it can be. Note that I said "can be" and

141

not "has to be." For the fact is people can be your greatest asset or a gigantic obstacle when it comes to turning new ideas into realities.

When you start trying to implement new ideas, you're probably going to run into difficult human roadblocks. It's naive to expect totally smooth sailing, and be thankful to the almighty if you do. The following are some of the more common human problems that you're likely to encounter along the way. The more you understand about these potential problems, the better equipped you'll be to recognize and successfully solve them, if they arise.

Resistance to Change

This is undoubtedly the largest and most likely people hurdle that you will encounter. As Morrie Brickman pointed out, "We're all in favor of progress, providing we can have it without change." Any new idea carries the seeds of change with it, and all of us have an innate tendency to resist change. Why? There are several answers.

Change is threatening. It's always accompanied by an obvious risk. It represents a venture from the known to the uncertainty of the unknown. Unfortunately many of us don't recognize the clinging to the "security" of the past and not changing often carries the most dangerous risk of all. The risk of change is obvious whereas the risk of not changing is covert. Someone once remarked, "Between grief and nothing, I'll take grief." Perhaps this best summarizes the feelings of those who resist change due to fear of the unknown.

People also resist change due to plain old inertia. We protect ourselves from the shock of change by clinging to familiar habits of the past. A classic example of this concerns the British army's use of a certain piece of artillery during the early days of World War II. The army was hard up for guns and a piece of formerly horse-drawn artillery was being used for coastal defense. It was a terribly slow-firing piece of equipment, and a time study consultant was hired to determine how the firing rate could be improved. After taking slow-motion pictures, the time-study man and his crew noticed something peculiar. Before firing the weapon, two members of the artillery crew stood perfectly still and came to attention for three seconds and held that position until the gun was fired. No one could understand why the men were supposed to stand at attention, until a very elderly colonel was consulted. At first, he was puzzled, but then he exclaimed, "I have it! They are holding the horses."

Change is resisted when people have an economic or social investment in the status quo. For example, if a sales representative is assigned a new territory, he may resist the idea because he fears a loss of income. Or he may feel comfortable with the relationships he has built with customers in the old territory. Resistance to change in organizations usually occurs because people fear losing contact with the ones they work with, or they fear being financially hurt or unemployed.

Change is resisted when people feel their status or self-image is threatened. John, a middle-aged executive, became enraged when his wife, Mary, announced she was going to seek outside employment after twenty years as a homemaker. Mary was bored and wanted something productive to occupy her days. Their son was in high school and a housekeeper handled most of the domestic chores. Although he raised numerous objections, John's real resistance to this change was that he perceived it as a threat to his status in the family. He had been reared to believe that it was a man's role to be the sole provider and having a working wife threatened his self-image of what a man should be.

Conformity—"Why Can't You Be Like Everyone Else?"

One of our strongest motivations is to be accepted by others, and this frequently translates itself into thinking and behaving like others. As Eric Hoffer observed, "When people are free to do as they please, they usually imitate each other."

Every day in hundreds of subtle and not so subtle ways, all of us are told to follow the rules, stay in line and conform to accepted norms of behavior. While this has definite advantages in a civilized society, conformity is all too often carried to extremes. Show me a dictator, and I'll show you someone who demands conformity.

Mignon McLaughlin remarked, "Every society honors its live conformists and its dead troublemakers." While not all troublemakers are creative, many creative people have been labeled in their time as revolutionaries, buffoons and enemies of society in general. While you probably aren't trying to implement a new idea that will change the world, you're still a likely candidate to encounter the conformity hurdle. In organizations, you can expect to be labeled a boat rocker if you try to innovate. Students who attempt to do creative work are frequently labeled "irresponsible" for not following the prescribed rules. Any idea that violates or changes accepted norms of behavior will likely bounce you against the barriers of conformity.

The easy way out is to follow the crowd, forget your ideas and be like everyone else. But to choose this path is to believe that someone else's opinion of you is more important than your opinion of yourself. In the final analysis, overconformity carries an exorbitant hidden price tag. First, it costs you your self-respect. And second, it doesn't deliver what it promises. People don't respect conformity. They respect strength.

Criticism

Critics gravitate toward new ideas in much the same way that rats gravitate toward civilization. I'm not referring to constructive critics who serve a useful purpose in the final stage of the creative process. Rather, I'm referring to criticism of the unconditional disregard variety. In this type of criticism you hear only what's wrong with your idea and why it isn't worth wasting time on.

It's one hell of a lot easier to criticize than it is to create, and this is why we have so many critics in the world today. The *critics are everywhere*. The truth is that many people who criticize only wish they had the courage to innovate, but their fear of failure immobilizes them. Focusing on their own inadequacies is much too painful. Consequently they choose to point out the flaws in others and their ideas. This soothes their conscience by giving themselves a false sense of superiority. As Richard Le Gallienne wrote, "A critic is a man created to praise greater men than himself, but he is never able to find them."

Another interesting thing about critics is that they are very quick to see and point out their own flaws in others. *Projection* is the name that psychologists give such behavior. A classic example of projection happened when my first book, *Working Smart*, was published. The overwhelming majority of reviews were positive and none of them panned the book. I was surprised at such a response. We all have different tastes. Consequently, I expected a mixture of positive and negative reviews. Finally, after *Working Smart* had been out about six months, some caustic and erroneous comments about it appeared in a book-review column. The reviewer heaped negative remarks on several self-help books and wrote, "Of all the make-an-extra-buck books, the soft-core psych titles are the most insidious, as they disguise their baser money interests behind the altruism of self-help." This sentiment against fast-buck exploiters of the public appeared in one of the national soft-core porno magazines! Reflecting on this experience, I was reminded of the wisdom of David Seabury, who wrote, "Freedom comes only from seeing the ignorance of your critics and discovering the emptiness of their virtue."

Cynicism

The previous story also illustrates cynicism, which is a special variety of criticism. Its purpose is to inflict guilt on the innovator. Whenever you have a new idea to implement, the cynic is the one who will say, "You're just out for yourself and don't care about the rest of us." Any action taken by others is reviewed in a negative light. As Evan Esar remarked, "The cynic who sneers at human nature is probably speaking from self-knowledge."

Cynics know the price of everything and the value of nothing. If you come up with an honest idea that brings you a lot of money or success, you're to be congratulated, not scorned. It proves that you've filled a need and helped a lot of people. You can't prosper without serving, and the greater your prosperity the better service you can provide in the future. In our society, people vote on the value of ideas with their dollars, and the public is a lot smarter than the cynics give them credit for. Unfortunately, the cynic's negative assumptions about people blinds him to this reality.

Envy

Plain old envy lies at the heart of much criticism and cynicism. All too often the people who discredit your ideas are thinking, "Why didn't I think of that?" or "I wish I had his ambition and courage" or "I wish I were that talented." Indeed, with the possible exception of imitation, envy is the sincerest form of flattery.

Like the majority of people hurdles, envy is a defensive reaction. Envious people try to shield themselves from their own feelings of inadequacy. They fail to realize that they are no more or less of a person because of the value of someone else's ideas or achievements. Consequently, they labor under the irrational belief that they can enhance their own self-worth by attacking the ideas or personality of others.

Another unfortunate thing about envy is that in addition to being a creative hurdle, it can destroy good relationships. All too often, close friends, relatives and colleagues are the first to become envious of a success or a potentially successful idea. The sad truth is that many of us handle success poorly, when it's someone else's. It seems almost paradoxical in our success-oriented society, but people who hit on sudden and large successes often speak of being deserted by those close to them.

Apathy

"Frankly, my dear, I don't give a damn," said the oft-quoted Rhett Butler. Just because you love your idea doesn't mean that others will. When people respond to your idea with indifference, it's usually for one of the following reasons:

1. It may be a disguised form of resistance to change, criticism, cynicism, envy—or any combination of them.
2. You haven't done a thorough job of presenting your idea in a manner that will enable others to grasp the value of it. (Refer to the last part of Chapter Six.)
3. Due to background, interests, and values this person simply isn't one who can get excited about your idea. If you

find yourself in such a situation, there's no point in trying to convince them. Simply move on and find those people who will support your idea. As Lin Yutang pointed out, "Nothing matters to the man who says nothing matters."

STRATEGIES FOR CLEARING THE PEOPLE HURDLES

According to W. C. Fields, "Horse sense is what a horse has that keeps him from betting on people." While you may tend to agree with that assessment of humanity when you're up against the people hurdles, it really isn't quite that hopeless. There are things you can do to reduce resistance to your ideas and up the odds that people will view them favorably. Certainly there are no guarantees when you're dealing with human beings. However, the following concepts can only help increase your chances of success.

Create a Need for Change

Getting someone to view your idea favorably is essentially one of changing their attitudes. In order for people to change, they first must become dissatisfied with the way things are. Thus, your first task is to create dissatisfaction, which can be done several ways.

1. You make people aware of the problems that currently exist and hope they will recognize the need to change and adopt your idea. If, for example, you're trying to convince your spouse of the need for buying a larger house or adding on to your present one, you could point out that growing children need their own room and that a lack of privacy is contributing to family disharmony.

2. You warn people about the hazards of nonchange. For several years, oil companies and governments have been trying to use this approach to convince Americans to change their energy-consumption habits. This approach paints a gloomy picture of the future if the status quo continues and tries to convince people to adopt new ideas or else.

3. You stress the benefits of change *to them*. People will only be motivated to adopt new ideas and change when they see it is in their own best interests to do so. Anything less will simply fall short in effectively getting them to change. Thus the benefits of your ideas have to be presented from their frame of reference rather than yours. Be empathetic. What's in it for them? For example, if you're trying to stress the benefits of conserving energy you might point out that using public transportation costs less than owning a gas guzzler and that smaller autos are easier to park.

A skillful imagineer usually can blend all three approaches to create a need for change. For example, if you're an executive trying to convince your company of the need for a computerized recordkeeping system, you could:

- Point out the wasted man-hours that are spent shuffling papers that could be done faster and better by computer.
- Remind them that they can almost surely count on contending with more paperwork in the future which will waste even more man-hours (and money) if the status quo is maintained.
- Stress the cost benefits and improved morale that will come from automating many of the paper-shuffling chores.

Similarly, if you're trying to convince your spouse to buy a house, you can use all three approaches. First, you show how all that rent money is going down the drain each month. Then you point out the fact that not buying today means you'll almost definitely pay more tomorrow, if you can afford it. And finally you could stress the benefits of having a tax shelter, hedge against inflation, personal freedom, equity and pride of ownership.

Some Other Hints for Reducing Resistance to Change

Creating dissatisfaction with the status quo is only one strategy that is helpful in getting new ideas adopted and implemented. The following are techniques that you may also find useful in overcoming resistance to new ideas and changes.

1. Meet resistance to change with openness and honesty. One of the greatest things you can do to reduce resistance to change is to remove the threat that it represents. All too often, change is viewed as threatening because people don't know the complete story. Unfortunately a vacuum of information is usually filled with half-truths, rumors and numerous inaccurate descriptions, all of which only results in more fear and resistance. Much of this can be prevented by making a concerted effort to keep people informed. Let them know what you have in mind, why it's beneficial and how it will affect them. Open and honest communication is a powerful antidote to the threat of uncertainty.

2. Involve people in the idea-development process and listen to their ideas. Research in organizations has found that resistance to new ideas and changes is significantly reduced when people are given the opportunity to participate in the change. Japanese managers are very skillful practitioners of this art. Whenever they are considering making a major change or decision, they withhold final judgment until everyone affected by their decision is consulted and allowed to express their views. While it takes them longer to reach a decision, the Japanese executives save time in the long run. The resistance to implementing their decisions is reduced because people feel they have had the chance to participate and express their views.

3. If possible, implement large changes on a gradual basis. Inasmuch as all of us are creatures of habit, the shock of radical changes is almost instinctively resisted. Therefore, the best way to implement most new ideas or changes is gradually, smoothly and systematically. This gives people the chance to become acclimated with minimum discomfort. In my time-management consulting practice, I give people numerous ideas for making better use of their time. Most ideas involve behavior changes. However, I warn them not to make a wholesale implementation of these ideas, because it usually results in frustration and failure. Instead I have them make a list of the techniques they feel would help them most and have them agree to implement only one new technique each week.

This reduces the shock of change and enables the new habits to become ingrained in a manner that will increase the odds of their lasting.

4. You also can reduce resistance to change by making tentative changes. Propose that the new idea be tried out for a short period of time or on a small scale to test its validity. For example, if you own a business and you would like to go to a four-day workweek or flexitime schedule, propose to your employees that you try it for a month or two. At the end of that time, people can be consulted to see how the idea is working. This gives your idea a fair test and lets people know that you're viewing any possible changes with an open mind and aren't emotionally attached to the idea for its own sake.

5. When people seem inclined to resist any changes, point out the fact that change and death are the only two certainties of the future. A very effective executive once told me, "I tell my employees that the only thing that never changes in our business is change." He could have just as accurately said that change is the only thing that we can depend on in our entire lifetime. Helping people become aware of the universality of change can help reduce their emotional attachments to the status quo.

6. Be reasonably certain that your new idea will be a definite improvement over the existing situation and isn't change simply for the sake of change. While all progress requires change, it's important to remember that not all change is progress. Moreover, change, like everything else in life, has a price attached to it. The price you pay for change is a temporary loss of stability and inconvenience while you and others are adapting to the change. Therefore, before embarking on new ideas, take into account the price involved and be reasonably certain it's worth the inconvenience. If people perceive you as one who makes wholesale changes for the sake of change, your ideas will be met with paramount resistance.

Expect to Be Criticized

When your new ideas and innovations come under fire, it only proves one thing. You're in there trying and not letting life pass you by. For that you should heartily congratulate yourself.

The fear of criticism and ridicule is one of our great creative cripplers. What's important to understand is that it isn't the criticism that's unpleasant but rather your negative reaction to it. Anytime your ideas are criticized, consider the source, the criticism and the motives of the critics. Who is criticizing? What are their qualifications? Why are they attacking your ideas? If your experience is anything like mine, you'll find that well over 90 percent of the time, what the critics say is irrelevant. If such is the case, ignore them and press on. Think about this: If what the critics have to say is so important, why is it that you'll never see a monument to one?

It's only natural to desire the approval of others, but the fact is you really don't need it. Weaning yourself from irrational needs for approval is a prerequisite for creative success. Instead of choosing to feel bad or become angry at your critics, realize that their reaction is a symbol of your growth and progress. What disturbs critics about your ideas is their problem, and one that only they can deal with. Concentrate your efforts on turning your ideas and goals into realities.

Few Presidents were criticized more in their time than Abraham Lincoln. His philosophy for dealing with criticism is one we can all profit by:

> . . . If I were to read, much less to answer all the attacks made on me, this shop might as well be closed for any other business. I do the very best I know how—the very best I can; and I mean to keep doing so until the end. If the end brings me out alright, what is said against me won't amount to anything. If the end brings me out wrong, ten angels swearing I was right would make no difference.

Obviously, not all criticism is destructive and useless. Keep an open mind for constructive criticism and strive to be objective when evaluating it. However, it's more important to doggedly believe in your ideas and be committed to them than it is to listen to the advice of critics, no matter how noble their intentions.

HOW TO BUILD A WINNING TEAM

Thus far we have discussed people in terms of the problems they can present when you're trying to be innovative. However, that's only one side of the coin. There are literally millions of people out there who can provide the help you need to turn your dreams into realities. No one in this world achieves anything totally by himself. We borrow ideas, time and energy from each other, and it's one of our roles as human beings to provide this help to each other. Your idea may call for building a team or network of people in order for it to be realized. If such is the case, here are some ideas for successful team building that will enable you to get the help and the results you seek.

1. Surround yourself with positive-thinking, goal-oriented people. This is extremely important. Feelings, attitudes and emotions all tend to be rather contagious when people are working together. While it's naive to believe that creative success is simply the result of positive thinking, it's also true that creative success begins with positive thinking. What you need are people possessing a "can do" attitude and an enthusiasm for life. Nothing succeeds like success, and positive people can create the necessary momentum to turn a small success into larger successes and so on. Seek out and surround yourself with those few who know why your idea will work and ignore the many who will tell you why it won't. As a writer I have had the good fortune of being surrounded by friends, editors, agents and numerous other people who have been very positive and enthusiastic about seeing my ideas published. Their encouragement and enthusiasm has been a major factor in motivating me to turn my ideas into realities. Without them, this book would have been nothing but a fleeting pipe dream.

2. Recruit the best people available. It almost never costs and almost always pays to go first class when it comes to hiring people for your idea team. The top people usually command top dollar but are almost always worth what they are paid. It's people, not things, that turn ideas into realities, and

your finished product will be a reflection of the people that help you produce it.

Bill and Betty learned this lesson the hard way. When hiring a contractor for the construction of their new home they simply chose the lowest bidder. Unfortunately, they got just what they paid for. After moving into the house they found a roof with several leaks, an unlevel foundation, faulty wiring that resulted in frequently blown fuses and generally shoddy materials and workmanship. Bargain-basement labor is usually anything but a bargain.

Most of us believe we can't afford to hire quality people. Before falling for that myth, ask yourself, "Can I afford not to hire the best?" It isn't what people cost that counts. It's what they're worth.

3. Let them do it their way. If you make the effort to get quality people on your team, you simply give them the ball and let them run with it. (Of course, I'm assuming that these people have the training and the tools to do the job.) Many a star performer will abandon an idea team if he feels constricted by the policies and dictums of others. Good people demand autonomy, latitude and the freedom to do the job their way. And because they're good they usually can find someone who will gladly meet their demands. This is particularly true when you're looking for people to do creative and nonroutine tasks.

A radio station once hired an announcer away from a competing station to write and produce radio spots. Brad was one of the top people in town and it took good money to get him. Unfortunately, after arriving at his new job, Brad found his creative abilities severely stifled. The program director insisted on rewriting and editing Brad's commercials so that they would conform with "station policy." The result was that Brad was no longer a creative force but merely a voice in the commercials. He felt his fresh ideas were being wasted and he soon departed for greener pastures.

4. Offer your team members goals that are challenging and meaningful to them. Once again it's important to realize that people can only be motivated from their own frame of reference and not someone else's. Every member of your team will be an individual having different values and needs. To the degree that you can be empathetic and perceive what moti-

vates a person, the more able you will be to set goals that are challenging and rewarding to them. It's also important to remember that people change, and what motivates someone today may not challenge them tomorrow. Ask yourself what this person is looking for today. What do they need? A sense of achievement? Money? Status? Recognition? Advancement? Freedom? Responsibility? Once you determine what motivates someone on your team, your basic job as a leader is to create a situation where they can satisfy their needs while contributing to the major goals of the team. Understanding another human being isn't totally possible, but your success as a leader will depend on how much understanding of others you can muster.

In his book *Human Behavior at Work*, Keith Davis tells a classic story of applied motivation. John was a mediocre assistant manager of a branch bank. He was always being transferred by bosses who wanted to unload him on another branch, and in eleven years of service he had served at eight branches. When he got to the ninth branch the manager decided to try and motivate him. He knew money wouldn't work because John had a comfortable inheritance and owned several apartment houses. Instead he came up with the idea of motivating John through recognition. To celebrate the branch's first birthday the manager held a party for all employees. He had a caterer prepare a large cake and write on top an important financial ratio which was under John's jurisdiction and happened to be favorable at the time. The result was that John was greatly moved by receiving this recognition, and his behavior substantially changed. Two years later he became the manager of another branch.

5. Give people the right to disagree. Any team needs good two-way communication. Coach Bear Bryant summarized this idea when he wrote:

> Over the years I've learned a lot about coaching staffs and one piece of advice I would pass on to a young head coach—or a corporation executive or even a bank president—is this: Don't make them in your image. Don't even try. My assistants don't look alike, think alike or have the same personalities. And I sure don't want them all thinking like I do. You don't strive for sameness, you strive for balance.

If people don't feel free to express themselves, the open climate for creativity and two-way communication will be hampered. A good team gets the maximum performance from each member, and this means they must feel free and uninhibited from intelligently expressing their views. You want thinking and committed people on your team—not "yes men." Some large companies have made high-level executives financially independent when promoting them to positions of great responsibility. The reasoning was that a financially independent person would be more inclined to speak and act freely if there were no fear of economic sanctions hanging over him.

6. Be lavish in your praise and recognition of your team members. People will work very hard if they know that sincere and honest achievement will be well recognized. Forget about personal status and glory. There's no limit to what can be done if you don't insist on getting the credit. In football, a smart running back is quick to point out the value of his offensive line. Every star needs a large supporting cast. See to it that your team members get the credit. The results they achieve will generate plenty of recognition for everyone.

This Taoist proverb says it best:

A wise man has a simple wisdom
Which other men seek.
Without taking credit
Is accredited.
Laying no claim
Is acclaimed.

When recognizing others for their contributions, be sure your compliments are specific. Don't simply remark that they're doing a good job. Point out what they do well, what you like best and why their contributions are valuable. "John's ability to come up with new ways for us to make money is his greatest asset. Last year he recommended we add four new products to our line, and all of them were winners. This talent combined with his capacity for tireless effort and company loyalty makes him an invaluable member of our team. Keep it up, John. We need all the winners we can get—and you're a winner." Which leads us to another important point.

Build the self-image of your teammates and your team. The bottom line of human performance is that people achieve according to what they believe. Those who believe they're winners and are on a winning team will perform like winners. Effective leaders are adept at capitalizing on this fact of human behavior.

Paul Dietzel, a young football coach at Louisiana State University in 1958, was one such leader. His young football team was picked to finish somewhere near the bottom of the Southeastern Conference. Of the first thirty-four players on the roster, none of them weighed over 210 pounds. In an attempt to motivate his players and instill pride, Dietzel broke his squad into three units and named them the White Team, Go Team and Chinese Bandits. On any other team, the players on the Chinese Bandits would have been the third string. However, Dietzel used them as defensive specialists and challenged them to live up to the tough and aggressive name he had given them. That year L.S.U. was undefeated, untied and was acclaimed the number-one team in both the Associated Press and United Press polls. On numerous occasions, the Chinese Bandits were sent into games and performed with an amazing dedication and brilliance that spelled the difference between victory and defeat. Looking back on that 1958 team some years later, Dietzel remarked, "Actually that 1958 team wasn't that good. But they never knew it."

7. Be enthusiastic and excited about your idea. If it's your dream and you aren't excited about it, why should anyone else be? Enthusiasm is contagious. What you feel and think about your ideas will be understood, if only intuitively, by everyone on your team. Enthusiastic, momentum-creating emotions must start at the heart of the idea team and reverberate like the ripples on a pond. As long as you're excited about your idea, you'll automatically be sending out the right vibes. Keeping your team enthusiastic, like charity, begins at home. Ideas for creating your own enthusiasm are discussed in Chapter Eleven.

A Word about Contacts

If you've ever tried to get a book, song, article or play published or if you've ever tried to get a lucrative job where there are numerous applicants, I don't have to tell you how tough it can be. Those who are successful generally will attribute their success to honest effort and being the best qualified. Those who don't succeed will frequently counter with the old cliché "It isn't what you know, it's who you know." Who's right? In their own way, both of them are.

Successful selling of your ideas is usually a combination of a good well-presented idea and whom you know. It isn't that talent and hard work are unimportant. It simply isn't enough. The fact is there are plenty of people with good ideas that don't pan out because they fail to come in contact with the right people who can provide the necessary help.

Because people are people, those in a position to dispense rewards will often prefer to give them to those they know rather than those they don't know. A known person represents a lesser risk. Political? You bet. Unjust? So what? Life is unjust. Accurate? Definitely. I didn't make the rules. But we all have to play by this one when the situation demands it. In a competitive society, creative success frequently hinges on being in contact with the right people at the right time. With that thought in mind, here are some ideas to guide you toward putting yourself in touch with those who can help.

1. Whom do you know? Much has been written about the importance of building an "old boy network" (or old girl network) in business. Talk with friends, associates and relatives about your idea. It's absolutely amazing who knows whom in this shrinking world of ours. They may be able to give you a direct introduction or at least a letter of referral to someone who is just the individual you're looking for. Better yet, the friend, relative or associate may be able to help you themselves.

2. If you are referred to someone who can't help you, ask them if they can suggest names of people who can. It's quite possible they may have a relative, friend or business associate who is looking for an idea like yours. It's amazing how many new and interesting people you can meet this way, and you're building a network of contacts that may be useful in the future. In this regard, it helps to keep a written record of all the people you meet. Someday you may be able to help them or refer someone else to them.

3. In addition to networking through friends, et cetera, start researching for people and organizations that could use your ideas. Read magazine and newspaper ads. As you listen to radio and watch television, keep a lookout for a possible opportunity. Libraries are usually filled with reference books that contain names, addresses and telephone numbers of people in industries and businesses that can help. Once you find a market for your idea, try to get specific names of people to contact. If you get this information, call them up and talk to them. Letters take time and can be ignored, but most people will succumb to the mystery of a long-distance telephone call. It may cost you a few dollars, but you could also be opening the door on something infinitely greater. Furthermore, a telephone call puts you in more personal contact with this person than a letter. If they can't help you, perhaps they can tell you the name of someone who can.

4. Don't be afraid to talk to strangers you meet. If you had a nickel for every idea that became a successful reality because of two people meeting each other by sheer chance, you would be a very wealthy person. We can only speculate on how many ideas have been turned into successes because the right two people bumped into each other on the street, met at a party or sat next to each other on an airplane. The point is that there are numerous people out there who can help you. How do you know that the stranger sitting next to you isn't one of them?

5. Go where the action is. When Willie Sutton was asked why he robbed banks, he replied, "Because that's where the money is." Similarly, to find the people that can help, you'll generally have to go to them. If you're expecting them to come to you, you're falling for the waiting-to-be-discovered myth. Frequently the people who can help you are concentrated in one or a few places. For example, New York is good for publishing, Houston for oil, Milwaukee for beer, and so on. Visit or move there and start building that ever-essential network.

When it comes to creative success, people can be an enormous obstacle, annoyance, essential ingredient or tremendous asset. How you treat them, teach them to treat you, and who you get to help you will be a determining factor in which role they play.

9

Situational Hurdles

*"Never underestimate the value of luck, but remember
that luck comes to those searching for something."*

—Stanley Marcus

IN ONE OF his classic posters, Tom Wilson's Ziggy remarked
that every time opportunity knocked, he was in the back taking out the garbage. One reason that poster is so successful is
that it echoes the sentiments of far too many of us. How many
success stories have you heard that never came to pass because the person telling it was suffering from excusitis? People suffering from this malady know why their idea could
have been successful and all the reasons it wasn't. How can
you tell when someone has excusitis? One sure way to recognize it is that the victim likes to play the blame game.

"My idea could have been a smash success if it weren't
for...

> the breaks
> a lack of money
> red tape
> God
> not knowing the right people
> my parents, spouse, children, in-laws, et cetera
> Uncle Sam
> being in the wrong place at the right time
> someone stealing my idea
> inexperience
> everything went wrong
> astrology."

The list of potential excuses is infinite, but the failure is attributed to other persons and situations.

Make no mistake about it. There are situations and circumstances that can raise havoc with your dreams as you try to turn them into realities. No doubt you'll encounter at least several of them along the way. However, the key to clearing the situational hurdles is to recognize those that are controllable by you and take steps to remove them, or better yet, prevent their occurrence.

One approach to dealing with situational hurdles is to recognize the many unconscious assumptions that you may be harboring about them. Many only exist in the mind and aren't really situational hurdles at all. Others are real, but you may be falsely assuming that there is nothing you can do to control them. Your assumptions can blind you to ways of bypassing them. In this chapter, we will examine some common problems that you're likely to bump into and what you can do about them. As you read these, bear in mind that the assumptions you make about the hurdles and your attitudes toward them will be the predominant factor in how well you succeed in overcoming them.

ARE YOU SURE IT'S A HURDLE?

All of us have an innate tendency to define problems outside ourselves, yet all too often the problem lies within. As Pogo once remarked, "We has met the enemy and they is us." What you may perceive as a situation limiting your achievement may not be the case at all. Your own preconceived notions or a lack of specific direction may be the problem. Or you may think you're spinning your wheels when, in fact, you are making steady progress. There are several things you should check before defining the problem as a situational one. While it's true that a well-defined problem is 80 percent solved, it's also true that an incorrectly defined problem is a waste of time and effort. Here are several things that can masquerade as situational hurdles and cause you to waste your time fighting ghosts.

Impatience

Things take time and creative success is no exception. Generally speaking, the greater the success you seek, the more time it's likely to take. Yet we live in a society of pushbutton need gratification where seemingly instant successes are paraded before our very eyes. Indeed, as Oren Arnold pointed out, the prayer of the modern American is "Dear God, I pray for patience. And I want it *right now!*"

Why do we demand instant everything? Because the promise of it is held out to us wherever we go. Just name your need and someone is out there promising to satisfy it pronto! Want to change your mood? We have pills to pick you up, bring you down, put you to sleep and keep you awake. If you want your appearance changed, you name it and it can be done. For the right price, you can even get a new face. If you don't like where you are, it's possible to be transported to the other side of the world in less than a day. Indeed, instant everything is the one common product of twentieth-century technology.

While I'm not advocating a return to the stone age (or even the nineteenth century), we should recognize that instant everything can erode our patience. And patience is the master key to any type of large success. It's important to know how to manage time (we will discuss that in Chapter Ten) but it's also important to realize this one fact: Given enough time, there's practically no limit to what can be accomplished. It took Michelangelo four years of painting on his back to complete the ceiling of the Sistine Chapel. Great cathedrals have taken centuries to complete. Biographies of great scientists are filled with numerous accounts of trying hundreds of experiments before succeeding. Thomas Edison and Madame Curie are cases in point.

Before assuming that you're up against some huge situational hurdles, first check your patience. Ask yourself, "Am I expecting too much too soon?" If so, step back, take a deep breath and keep plugging away. Most of us simply give up too soon. As Arnold Glasgow put it, "The key to everything is patience. You get the chicken by hatching the egg—not by smashing it."

Poorly Defined Goals

The need for having a system of well-thought-out goals was discussed in Chapter Two. Do you have a plan that makes every day count, or do you have the feeling that each day brings only frustration and fatigue? People who feel that they're spinning their wheels and getting nowhere are often frustrated not because of the situation but rather because of a lack of purpose.

Bob was a state university professor who fancied himself as a very hard worker. He put in long hours on numerous research projects, which for the most part were unrecognized. His lack of meaningful achievement left him frustrated, fatigued and ill-tempered. Students avoided his classes like the plague and colleagues found him abrupt and difficult to work with. Bob blamed his problems on lazy students, an inflexible university administration and the refusal of colleagues to co-operate. A closer look, however, revealed that Bob's work contained a lot of motion and little or no direction. His students were given frequent and lengthy assignments of questionable value. His research efforts were unrelated to each other and had no orientation toward a higher goal that could ultimately give him the recognition he sought. Instead of concentrating his efforts on a book or a long-range research topic, he chose to do numerous small studies on unrelated topics. He was so involved in studying different things that he never became a recognized expert in any one thing. In short, Bob was caught in the activity trap. Convinced that he was in the wrong place, he went to another university only to encounter the same problems and frustrations. What Bob perceived as situational hurdles was really a lack of personal direction.

Check your goals out before deciding that your main problem is a situational one. Are the goals specific, measurable and accompanied with target dates? Are they realistic? Are they *your* goals? Have you changed your goals? Are they compatible with each other? Has the situation changed to make them no longer feasible? Are you doing something each day, no matter how small, to move you closer to achieving your most important goal? Considering the answers to these questions can keep you from falling into the activity trap and spinning your wheels over an incorrectly defined problem.

Disorganization

A routine of chaotic work habits is another demon that can hinder your progress. No doubt there are many creative, successful people who are terribly disorganized. The reason they are successful is that they know what they're trying to achieve and pursue their goals every day. They probably don't have the formal system of goals outlined in Chapter Two, but they do have an overall sense of direction and commitment. It's far more important to have the proper goals than to be properly organized. Given the right goals, proper organization increases your efficiency. Given the wrong goals, proper organization only enables you to do the wrong thing very well.

Just what is proper organization? Running around with a stopwatch, keeping a clear desk and becoming a compulsive efficiency nut? Not at all. Good organization means choosing a proper work environment, getting the proper training and tools to do the job and arranging things in a way that will enable you to be comfortable and have easy access to the tools you need. It's a very personal thing and each individual should organize himself in accordance with the job being done and his own personality. You're well organized if you can put your hands on whatever you need whenever you need it. If you spend a lot of time searching for things, or if you find yourself frequently losing things, you have a definite problem with disorganization and need to give some conscious thought to rectifying it.

An Overwhelming Problem or Goal

It's terribly easy to make excuses and find all sorts of real and imaginary barriers to achieving your goal if you perceive the project as an overwhelming one. Don't psych yourself out by falling into this trap. Most major projects look overwhelming at the outset. This prevents more good ideas from becoming realities than anything else. It causes people to throw in the towel without even trying or, worse yet, make a defeatist effort.

The key to any type of major success is to break large projects down into numerous minor tasks and tackle them one at a time. A home is built with the addition of each new brick. A business is built with the addition of each new customer. Movies are made one scene at a time. Sports championships are made one play at a time. As Robert Schuller puts it, "Inch by inch anything's a cinch." Eric Sevareid refers to this strategy as the principle of the "next mile" and proclaims it to be some of the best advice he has ever received. The following is part of what he had to say in an article in *Reader's Digest:*

> During World War II, I and several others had to parachute from a crippled army transport plane into the mountainous jungle on the Burma-India border. It was several weeks before an armed relief expedition could reach us, and then we began a painful, plodding march "out" to civilized India. We were faced by a 140-mile trek, over mountains, in August heat and monsoon rains.
>
> In the first hour of the march I rammed a boot nail deep into one foot; by evening I had bleeding blisters the size of a 50-cent piece on both feet. Could I hobble 140 miles? Could the others, some in worse shape than I, complete such a distance? We were convinced we could not. But we *could* hobble to that ridge, we *could* make the next friendly village for the night. And that, of course, was all we had to do....
>
> When I relinquished my job and income to undertake a book of a quarter of a million words, I could not bear to let my mind dwell on the whole scope of the project. I would surely have abandoned what has become my deepest source of professional pride. I tried to think only of the next paragraph, not the next page and certainly not the next chapter. Thus, for six solid months, I never did anything but set down one paragraph after another. The book "wrote itself."
>
> Years ago, I took on a daily writing and broadcasting

chore that has totaled, now, more than 2000 scripts. Had I been asked at the time to sign a contract "to write 2000 scripts" I would have refused in despair at the enormousness of such an undertaking. But I was only asked to write one, the next one, and that is all I have ever done.*

Another antidote to conquering overwhelming tasks is to realize that with most major projects, the hardest part is getting started. The most difficult part of writing a book is creating a solid outline and the second hardest part is to write the first paragraph. Writing is time consuming but if you have a good plan and get a fast start, it isn't very difficult. People who have amassed fortunes invariably will tell you that the hardest part is accumulating that first few thousand dollars to invest. Promise yourself you'll take that first difficult step before talking yourself out of getting whatever you really want. Chop that big task up into little pieces and take the first bite. You'll thank yourself for it later on.

CLEARING THE REAL SITUATIONAL HURDLES

The fact that you know your goal, have the patience of angels, are well organized and aren't overwhelmed by your ambitions (if this describes you, you're disgustingly well adjusted) doesn't immunize you from situational obstacles. All of us are prey to strange and numerous forces that can slow down or prevent the realization of our dreams. However, the fact that they exist outside of you doesn't necessarily make them outside of your control. Here are some of the more common situational hurdles you may run into and some strategies for successfully clearing them.

*Eric Sevareid, "The Best Advice I Ever Had," *Reader's Digest*, vol. 70, no. 420 (April 1957), p. 140.

Luck

Obviously luck is an asset or an obstacle, depending on which type you get. But just what is luck anyway? Bad luck is best described by what has become known to many as Murphy's Law. Although there are numerous versions, here is one version of Murphy's Law and ten of the most popular corollaries:

If anything can go wrong, it will.

Corollaries:

1. Nothing is as easy as it looks.
2. Everything takes longer than you think.
3. If there is a possibility of several things going wrong, the one that will cause the most damage will be the one to go wrong.
4. If you perceive that there are four possible ways in which a procedure can go wrong, and circumvent these, then a fifth will promptly develop.
5. Left to themselves, things tend to go from bad to worse.
6. Whenever you set out to do something, something else must be done first.
7. Every solution breeds new problems.
8. It is impossible to make anything foolproof because fools are so ingenious.
9. Nature always sides with the hidden flaw.
10. Mother Nature is a bitch.

If that isn't a vivid enough description of bad luck in action, consider O'Toole's commentary on Murphy's Law: "Murphy was an optimist."

On the other hand, good luck is an entirely different matter. Have you ever stopped to consider just what good luck actually is? It's opportunity meeting preparation. In one sense, life is a series of good and bad breaks. However, lucky people prepare themselves to capitalize on opportunities and take steps to minimize their losses in case misfortune strikes. Can a person improve his luck? Yes, and probably more than you think. Here are some things you can do to make things break your way:

1. Get to know the circumstances surrounding the opportunities you want and keep your tools ready. An opportunity that you aren't prepared to capitalize on is useless. For example, if your goal is to make money in the stock market or real estate, you prepare by knowing the market so you can recognize opportunities and have access to the capital to invest when a good deal comes along. Lucky people are ready to strike when the iron is hot. And they don't hesitate to do so.

2. Be alert for serendipity. Horace Walpole wrote a story of the princes of Serendip who had the knack of making unexpected discoveries they weren't looking for. Hence, the word *serendipity* was coined. The essence of serendipity is to stumble on to some useful opportunity or discovery totally by accident. Instead of writing off an accidental happening as irrelevant, look for the possibility that it may present an opportunity that can move you toward achieving your goals. Many creative discoveries and solutions to problems are made this way. For example, Dr. Alexander Fleming was examining a culture plate that became contaminated with mold. As he looked at the culture under the microscope, he saw colonies of bacteria, looking like islands surrounded by clear spaces. Fleming reasoned that the mold might be preventing the spread of bacteria, and this observation led to the discovery of penicillin. A lucky discovery? Perhaps, but how many other biologists given the same culture would have dismissed the observation as irrelevant?

3. Make it a point to cultivate new friendships. The necessity for contacts and how to make them was discussed in Chapter Eight, so I won't belabor the point. The more friends you have, the greater number of opportunities you'll encounter. Lucky people are almost always gregarious and friendly. They enjoy others and because of this they radiate a personal magnetism that draws people to them.

4. Make your own breaks. Most of us sit around waiting for things to break for us. Good luck, but don't bet on it. Your chances of success are much greater if you take things into your own hands and go directly after what you want. No better example of this exists than that of Dr. Wayne Dyer. In 1976 Dyer had written a book entitled *Your Erroneous Zones*. At the time, he was a relatively unknown professor and no spectacular success was expected from the book. Dyer didn't

see it that way, however, and set out to make his book the nation's No. 1 best seller. Instead of complaining about the lack of publicity and promotion the publisher gave his book, Dyer took the matter into his own hands. He bought several hundred copies of his book, loaded them into his car and set out to educate America about the wonderful book he had written. Over a six-month period, Dyer personally delivered between fifteen and sixteen thousand copies of his book to bookstores. His travels covered twenty-eight thousand miles and forty-seven states. In the process, he gave approximately eight hundred publicity interviews and insisted that feature writers and interviewers hear him out. Due to his valiant efforts, *Your Erroneous Zones* became the No. 1 best seller and made Dyer one of the world's most acclaimed authors. It's only fitting that his next book was entitled *Pulling Your Own Strings*.

5. Pay close attention to your hunches. The importance of hunches in the illumination stage of creativity was mentioned earlier. However, in addition to providing creative insight, hunches can point the way to opportunity. Very often hunches are a collection of facts stored at the subconscious level. Before deciding to trust a hunch, ask yourself, "Is it possible that I've managed to gather information about this without consciously realizing it?" If so, pay strong attention to it. As James Stephens remarked, "What the heart knows today, the head will understand tomorrow." Never trust hunches for things such as card games, slot machines and raffles. And another word of caution: Never confuse your hunches with wishful thinking. It's easy to confuse bad hunches and strong wishes.

6. You must be willing to take calculated risks. J. Paul Getty was considered by many to be lucky. He founded his fortune in oil at age twenty-three. However, he gambled on drilling wells and won. Said Getty, "There's always an element of chance and you must be willing to live with that element. If you insist on certainty, you will paralyze yourself."

7. Minimize your losses. Lucky people get out of bad situations before they become worse. It's been said that the key to being successful in the stock market isn't in knowing when to buy but when to sell. If things seem to be on a definitely bad

skid, get out while you can. As an anonymous source put it, "If you're losing a tug-of-war with a tiger, give him the rope before he gets to your arm. You can always get another rope."

8. Head Murphy off at the pass. One reason lucky people are lucky is that they never depend on it. They're aware of the fickleness of fortune and know that bad luck has to be prepared for just like opportunity. J. Paul Getty remarked, "When I go into any business deal, my chief thoughts are on how I'm going to save myself if things go wrong." While you must take calculated risks to be lucky, this doesn't prevent you from having a contingency plan if things sour. Never make the mistake of assuming that good fortune will bail you out. Have a backup plan just in case.

9. Don't fall into the justice trap. All of us have been conditioned to expect and look for justice in our lives. Teachers, lawyers, judges, politicians and clergymen advocate justice for all. It's a great idea but it's also a myth. Justice doesn't exist. While you may argue that there is an ultimate justice in the hereafter, that's a point I'll leave for the philosophers and theologians to ponder. The fact is that in the here and now justice, like beauty, only exists in the eye of the beholder. Despite the greatest efforts of governments, clergymen, judges and the like, life isn't fair and never will be. In some way almost every person you meet will in some way be more fortunate and less fortunate than you. I don't mean for this to be a cynical look at life but rather an accurate portrayal of the way things are. Some people are born to great wealth and others to poverty. That's not fair. Some people have strong bodies and others are maimed or handicapped. That's not fair. Older people and minorities are discriminated against in the job market and that's not fair. The list of injustices in this world is infinite.

The problem with the justice trap is that it lulls us into believing that life owes us fair treatment, when in fact life owes us nothing. Those of us who fall into the justice trap usually tend to become immobilized when life shortchanges us. This prevents us from pouncing on future opportunities. Don't let that happen. Learn from your misfortunes and resolve to not let them stop you from realizing your dreams. Wallowing in self-pity and lamenting over your bad breaks is one sure way to court future misfortunes.

Money

How many good ideas have died on the drawing board because of that age-old excuse "We don't have the money"? The problem really isn't a lack of money. The people who say this have just prematurely turned off their dream machines. Just because you don't have money doesn't mean you can't get the capital you need to start your idea on its way to realization. There are all sorts of options to obtaining the funding you need no matter how much money you're talking about. Good ideas attract money the same way that honey attracts bees. If you make a concerted effort to come up with the capital you need, you can find it. Use some of the idea-generating techniques that were discussed earlier to solve the problem of raising money for your pet idea. The following are some common ways that have been used by others to clear the money hurdle. Perhaps one or more of these will work for you.

1. Don't be afraid to borrow money. There's no getting around the fact that it takes money to make money. However, no one said it has to be your money. Some people are absolutely petrified of debt, and this kills many a good idea. While I don't advocate frivolous borrowing, remember that there is a very positive side to borrowing. First, it benefits you by allowing you the chance to realize your dream. Second, it benefits the users of your dream by making your product or service a reality. And third it benefits the lender who gets to make a return on the excess capital he has invested in your idea. There are all sorts of people with plenty of cash looking for good ideas to invest in. Seek them out and tell them about your idea. Henry Ford started his business without investing a penny of his own money.

2. You also can raise money by selling off tangible assets that you own. My good friend Denny Had parlayed this strategy into a multimillion-dollar business. In 1974 Denny was a stockbroker who dreamed of owning his own electronics manufacturing company. In August 1974 Denny quit his job and began the Dentron Radio Company in his basement. In order to acquire $10,000 necessary capital, Denny sold all tangible

assets he owned that were not necessary for providing for the welfare of his family. The family cars were sold and replaced with bicycles. Stocks were sold. "Look around," says Denny. "It's amazing what really isn't a necessity for a happy family life." Denny got a lot of raised eyebrows from friends and relatives who thought he had flipped out. However, it only took Denny fourteen months to convert that $10,000 into $1,000,000 in revenue. And it only took him three months to replace the family cars with better cars. Today, Dentron is a multifaceted manufacturing and marketing operation that sells electronic equipment worldwide. As for Denny, he just keeps dreaming, and Dentron keeps growing . . . and growing . . . and growing.

3. You can raise funds through numerous schemes. Hold a raffle. Throw a dance or a dinner. Have a garage sale. The number of different types of fund-raising events you can hold is almost limitless. And all of them can contribute to your attaining the amount of money you need. I recently heard that someone raised $1,000 by raffling off his $200 paycheck!

Before becoming a film star, W. C. Fields came up with a novel way to make money by "working" as a professional drowner in Atlantic City. He would swim into the ocean, pretend to drown and be rescued by a lifeguard. As he was being revived, beach vendors would sell hot dogs and soft drinks to the gathering crowds, and Fields later collected a percentage of the profits.

4. Another alternative is to consider moonlighting as a money-raising source. However, I only recommend this as a last resort. If you're trying to innovate, you'll want to concentrate your time and energy on turning your dream into a reality. Second jobs are time-consuming and when it comes to creativity, time is much more important than money.

One final word of caution about money matters. If your dream is an artistic endeavor, such as making a recording or having a book published, beware of those who offer you a recording or book contract on the condition that you put up some of your own money. Legitimate record and publishing companies don't operate that way. If the company is on the level and likes your work, they will pay you for granting them the right to sell your work to the public. Beware of any operation that praises your talents and then asks for money. There are plenty of them out there.

Inexperience

It's been said that the trouble with experience is that you never have it until after you need it. Indeed, experience is the one thing that none of us are born with. Yet the lack of experience is a most common situational hurdle. Actually there are two types of hurdles that can be attributed to inexperience. The first is external. You're denied opportunities because you lack experience. Practically everyone is caught in the "want a job, get some experience, want some experience, get a job" dilemma when they are young. The ideas and skills of the experienced and proven winners are almost always given preference over those of the new and untried.

The second type of inexperience hurdle is internal. It's actually a spinoff of the old perfectionism problem. In effect, we tell ourselves, "I've never tried anything like this before. Better abandon this idea before I make a fool of myself." You overcome this type of hurdle by giving yourself the luxury of doing a poor job. A successful businessman once remarked, "Give me a young man with brains enough to make a fool of himself." There's a lot of wisdom contained in that statement. You had to learn to crawl before you walked, and you, no doubt, fell down numerous times in the process of trying. Don't immobilize yourself over the fear of being bad. It's one price of creative success. Write a lousy poem. Sing off key. Build a poorer mousetrap. I've heard successful comedians say that one key to success is to have some place to begin where you can be bad. If you're inexperienced, remember that anything worth doing is worth doing poorly. So get in there, make your mistakes and learn from them. As John Barrymore wisely noted, "You can only be as good as you dare to be bad."

The external inexperience hurdle is another problem. You're faced with the task of proving to others that you're worthy of opportunity. There are several options to clearing this obstacle:

1. You can volunteer to work for someone at no pay for the privilege of learning and gaining experience. John, a high school student, did this. He wanted to break into radio broadcasting but found it almost impossible to get a job without experience. He talked a local radio-station manager into letting him work at night answering the telephone and filing records. Eventually, the time came when John was allowed to work as a weekend announcer, and from this initial experience he launched a career in radio.

2. Credentials can somewhat compensate for a lack of experience. Any way that you can demonstrate competence or knowledge about what you want to do will help. The person with proper credentials always has the edge on the person without them when it comes to opportunities. I can use myself as an example here. When I set out to write my first book I had no experience as an author, and as you may know, getting a first book published can be terribly difficult. However, I did have a Ph.D. in Management and experience as a seminar leader and consultant in time management. No doubt, these credentials helped me secure several offers from publishers for *Working Smart*.

3. By all means, if you're experienced, you must radiate self-confidence, enthusiasm and a willingness to learn. Most of us enjoy helping an eager, ambitious person realize his dreams and if you project an enthusiastic, can-do spirit, you'll greatly up the odds of getting that break you need. No matter what doubts you have about your abilities, this is not the time to confess them. The message you want to get across tactfully is "I know where I'm going and sooner or later I'll get there. I'm eager to learn and know that I have what it takes."

4. Play the role. Dress and behave like someone who has experience in the endeavor you seek. Actors frequently live the life-styles of people they're going to portray in order to give a more convincing performance. Why not take a tip from the thespians and try this yourself. Every group of people has certain norms of dress and behavior. Whether you want to be a performer, executive, artist, hairstylist or whatever, meet some of these people and take note of the way they dress, think and behave. Do they use special buzz-words or have their own vocabulary? Learn the vocabulary and use it. Do they congregate at special places? Go there and talk to them.

Do they have any special-interest groups or professional associations? Join them. Do they have a particular style of dress? Dress like them. The point is as you assume the role of an experienced professional you will begin to think and act like one. The result is that people will tend to think of you as "their kind of person" and be more likely to offer you the break you're looking for. While overconformity can hamper creativity, a certain amount of conformity is necessary to secure opportunity. Once you get your foot in the door, you'll get plenty of chances to express your own ideas. Role playing can also be a great confidence builder. Who knows? You may buy your own act!

PART IV

FOLLOWING
THROUGH TO
SUCCESSFUL REALITY

10

Learning to Use Time

*"Time, like a snowflake, disappears while we're trying to
decide what to do with it."*

—St. Louis *Bugle*

WHAT A STRANGE and precious resource time is. All of us are
given a certain amount of time but we don't know how much
we have until it's all gone. We talk about saving time and
killing time when actually we can't do either. We have no
choice but to spend it at a constant and flowing rate—sixty
minutes per hour, twenty-four hours per day, three hundred
sixty-five days per year. Indeed, more often than not the difference between creative success and failure lies in the ability
of the innovator to effectively manage his or her time.

Stop for a moment and think about people you know who
have successfully reached their goals and turned their dreams
into realities. Although there may be numerous reasons why
any one of them succeeded, all of them probably had one
factor in common. They knew how to use their time to get
things done. You can't save time, but there are numerous options available as to how you may spend it. Choose the right
ones and you'll reach your dreams. Choose the wrong ones
and you'll be a dreamer.

Many people shy away from any thoughts about managing
time. The idea sounds threatening and freedom restricting.
They visualize keeping track of every minute, running around
with a stopwatch and being forever busy as the indicators of
good time management. As one who has written a book on the
subject, served as a time-management consultant, and conducted numerous seminars and workshops, I can assure you
that good time management is anything but that. Good time
management means *making* the time to do the things that are

most important to you. Good time management increases your freedom rather than restricting it. Through good time management you reach your goals by working smarter rather than harder. And as a result you will see your ideas turned into realities faster and with less frustration and fatigue.

If you made the effort to set the long-range and intermediate goals using the exercises in Chapter Two, you're well on your way to effective time management. Setting goals and priorities is at the heart of it all. However, there are other important techniques that you can use to make the most of every day. These concepts are simple, easily applicable and, best of all, they work. Let's look at a few of them. When you're trying to make things happen you'll find these ideas invaluable.

STRIVE TO BE EFFECTIVE, NOT BUSY

If being busy was the key to managing time, most Americans wouldn't have any time management problems. But alas, such is not the case. We're a hyped-up, on-the-move group of people who are always rushing to get from one place to another. Why are we that way? One reason is that many of us confuse activity with results. Yet, ironically, people have a tendency to be most busy when they are least confident in their abilities or goals. How many times have you heard "Look busy, the boss is coming"?

Effectiveness, doing the right job, is the goal of time management. It means, above all, knowing what results you're seeking. Until you know what you want, it makes little difference how hard you work, how busy you are, or how efficiently you're doing the job. As Thoreau remarked, "It isn't enough to be busy. Ants are busy. The question is 'What are we busy about?'" Being effective and being busy are two separate things. Being effective means investing your time on the few activities that are most important to you and pursuing them at a comfortable pace. Being busy is a ticket to wheel spinning and subsequent frustration.

TOOLS FOR UNDERSTANDING AND MANAGING YOUR USE OF TIME

Do you know where your time goes? You probably answered yes. Have you ever tried keeping a written record of how you spend your time? You probably said no. One key to understanding time usage is that it's mostly a matter of habit. We tend to do certain things every day without thinking and most of this behavior makes for good use of time. Think of how much time you would waste if you had to stop and think about everything you do. However, a lot of habits are needless patterns of behavior that waste time. Most of us are unaware of our habits until we make the effort to observe and record them. We think we know where our time goes when, in fact, few of us really do. The following idea will help you under-stand how you're using time.

Keep a Time Log Periodically

Before you panic and assume I'm asking you to turn yourself into an automaton, accounting for every second of your life, let me assure you that I'm not. Instead, try this for one week:

1. Make a list of about thirty activities that you commonly perform in an average week. You may find it helpful to classify them into categories such as job activities, personal activities, family activities, leisure activities and so on. Be sure to include a miscellaneous category.

2. After making this list, estimate how much time you think you spend each week on each activity. Round it off to the nearest half-hour and write it down.

3. For one week record how you spend the bulk of each half-hour in terms of the thirty activities you've listed.

4. At the end of the week, compare your actual use of time with your estimated use of time. No doubt, you'll find some real surprises. Now that you know where your time is going, be very honest with yourself and write down the answers to these questions:

- How did I waste time? What can be done to prevent or reduce wasted time in the future?
- How did I waste other people's time? Whose time did I waste? How can I prevent this from happening?
- What activities am I now performing that can be reduced, eliminated or given to someone else to do?
- What did other people do that wasted my time? Can anything be done to reduce or eliminate future occurrences? If so, what?
- What did I do that was urgent but unimportant?
- What did I do that was important in light of my goals?
- Am I spending my time pursuing those things that are important to me? If not, why not? If so, how?
- Starting today, I'm going to do the following things to make better use of my time . . .

The time log and answers to those questions will give you a much greater understanding of where your time is going and how you can make better use of it. It's a good idea to do the time log exercise once every six months. It helps you uncover new time wasters before they become ingrained. It's easier the second time around, and moreover you'll probably see an improvement in your use of time, if you've made a conscious effort at improving.

Set Daily Goals

In Chapter Two, I pointed out the need for setting long-range and intermediate goals, complete with target dates for achievement. One of the most powerful time-management strategies is to set daily goals which contribute to the attainment of longer-range goals. Daily goals are set by making a to-do list. Every day, either at the beginning of the day or at the end of the previous day, make a list of things you want to accomplish and rank them in order of importance. Keep this list on one piece of paper and take it wherever you go. This one positive habit will repay you many times over.

When Charles Schwab was president of Bethlehem Steel he asked a consultant for advice on how to make better use of his time. The consultant told Schwab to write down the six most important tasks he had to do each day and rank them in order of importance. "Don't be concerned if you have only finished one or two," said the consultant to Schwab. "If you can't finish them all by this method, you couldn't have by any other method either; and without some system you'd probably not even decided which was the most important." Several weeks later Schwab sent the consultant a check for $25,000 and proclaimed the advice to be the most profitable he had ever followed.

Don't feel guilty about not getting everything done on your to-do list. Just be sure you get the most important items done. The 80/20 Rule applies here. Eighty percent of the value of a to-do list is contained in 20 percent or less of the items. Concentrate on doing first things first and you'll see a wholesale increase in your effectiveness. If you only get to the one or two most important items, you're probably making much better use of your time than most of us.

Schedule a Quiet Time Every Day

You need time each day to be alone with your thoughts. This gives you the chance to consider your goals, make your to-do list and decide how you're going to use the day to move you closer to your goals. Even if you can only spare ten minutes each day, be sure to take them. It's a wise investment of time that may salvage you from the activity trap. You can also use quiet time for meditating or creative thinking.

Many successful executives know the value of quiet time. They schedule their day to arrive at the office an hour or two before the regular workday begins. During this period of peace and tranquillity they can consider important decisions or do solitary work free from distractions and interruptions. Because they arrive early, they can usually leave early and get an added bonus by reducing commuting time. Wasted time in traffic jams is eliminated.

Some companies have established a quiet-hour policy with success. For the first hour of each working day, everyone works alone. Telephone calls aren't made or accepted and everyone works on their most important tasks and plans the remainder of the day. Meetings and drop-in visits are likewise ruled out during the quiet hour. It's an interesting concept, and if you work for a company (or own one) you may wish to suggest trying it. If you can't afford a quiet hour, how about a quiet half-hour?

Capitalize on Your Prime Time

Another powerful time-management technique is to take the most important tasks you have to do and perform them at the time of day when you're at your best. Making the most of prime time enables you to do things more effectively and with less effort. Schedule the routine and less important items for a time when your level of physical and mental energy isn't as high.

All of us go through subtle changes in our moods and abilities each day. For most of us, our best time is usually between 10 A.M. and 2 P.M., but this certainly isn't universal. Some people are morning glories and others are night owls. Another interesting facet of prime time is that what is prime time for one activity isn't necessarily prime time for another. For example, you might be at your best for creative thinking in the morning, physical activities in the afternoon and socializing in the evening. As a writer I've found the prime-time concept invaluable. I do my best idea-generating early in the morning and my best writing in the afternoons. Therefore I decide what to write about first thing in the morning and jot down notes to myself. Then I take care of other daily chores until the afternoon, when I write. It's a schedule that makes for productive and enjoyable writing. Along with the daily to-do list, capitalizing on your prime time is one of the most valuable time management tools. It isn't the hours that you put in your work that counts. It's the work you put in your hours.

For Flexible Scheduling, Stay Loose

Overscheduling and overorganizing your day is a blueprint for frustration and fatigue. A tight schedule is built on the assumption that everything's going to go just as planned. And few, if any, days ever go exactly as planned. It's a good rule of thumb to never schedule more than half your day. The only way to keep the unexpected from raising havoc with your schedule is to budget time for it. Murphy and his friends thrive on tight schedules. If you think a task will take an hour to complete, give yourself an hour and fifteen minutes. If you're unfamiliar with the task, give yourself an hour and a half.

One key to creative success is to be able to block out large amounts of uninterrupted time. This allows you to invest your energies in the important goals with high payoffs. Scheduling for important tasks is best done on paper using a daily desk calendar or weekly planner. Be sure to give yourself deadlines for achieving these goals and schedule time to pursue them in the following manner:

1. Determine the deadline target date and mark it on your schedule.

2. Estimate the total number of hours you will need to reach your goal. Remember Murphy. Everything takes longer than you expect.

3. Once you've determined how much time a task will take, work back from the deadline and block off some hours to devote to the task. This will also tell you the latest possible date you can expect to start the task and successfully meet the deadline.

Make Time For You

Doggedly pursuing a task and filling up every hour with hard work can be very self-defeating. This is especially true of creative work. Unless you make the effort to get away and let your subconscious work, you aren't allowing the incubation stage of the creative process to take place. You force yourself into a rut which can prevent you from finding simpler, better and more enjoyable ways to get things done. Worse yet, workaholism can be hazardous to your health. Numerous tales of alcoholism, divorce, nervous breakdowns, ulcers and coronaries are characteristic of the workaholic. As an anonymous philosopher once observed, "A rut is a grave with the end knocked out."

You find the time for recreation and diversion the same way that you find time for everything else. You make it. There is always time to do the important things in life, and diversion is one of the most important. Get yourself some hobbies or activities that can allow you to mentally and physically escape from your work. When you return to your tasks, you'll find that you will pursue them with much more vigor and zeal.

You may also find it helpful to have large amounts of idle, unplanned time. Such a recommendation borders on heresy in our busy, busy, hurry-up world. Most of us feel terribly guilty about not having anything to do. However, despite whatever you may have been taught, there's nothing inherently wrong with doing nothing. I do nothing rather frequently and enjoy it immensely. So what? It hurts no one and those are the times when I get some of my best ideas. Best of all it prevents me from becoming a slave to the clock and feeling oppressed when there's something important to do.

Get the Most from Already-Committed Time

If you make the effort to keep a time log or make a weekly schedule and block out time for the essentials, you'll quickly realize that a great deal of your time is already committed. Most of us work eight hours per day, commute two hours per day and sleep another eight hours per day. Add numerous family and social obligations such as shopping, mealtime, and personal grooming and there's precious little time to call your own. However, with a little forethought you can get some extra mileage out of those already committed hours. Tape recorders, reading material and note pads are the tools most frequently used to get the most out of committed time. While waiting for the doctor, dentist or hair stylist you can write or dictate letters, update your to-do list or plan a major project. Better yet, you can use the time for creative exercise and problem solving. Always carry essential reading material with you to capitalize on spare moments. Of course, you can simply use the time to relax or meditate.

I know one executive who commutes several hours per day and makes it a habit to keep a tape recorder in the car. He uses the time to dictate letters and memos and listen to tapes about subjects that interest him. I also know an astute sales representative who capitalizes on traveling time between customers using a recorder. After calling on a customer, she uses the time in travel to record whom she just visited, what they discussed and what business was transacted. Six months later, before she goes to call on that same customer, she plays back the tape. Her customers are astounded by her ability to remember details! Another sales representative I knew was working on an M.B.A. degree at night. He used travel time for studying. First he records his notes on a cassette after each class. He would then listen to them while traveling between customers.

Shopping time can be a real time consumer. The best way to deal with this type of committed time is to minimize it by shopping when everyone else isn't. Avoid supermarkets and shopping centers on weekends and banks at lunchtime. If possible, arrange your schedule to shop during weekdays or evenings and do your banking in the morning. If you find yourself stuck in line, be prepared by having something to do. Carry a list of problems needing creative solutions and use that time to think up ideas and jot them on a note pad. While in line you can also knit, do isometric exercises, read, or make a list of people to invite to your next party.

Most of us think of time in terms of hours, days and weeks. It's the lifetimes and the minutes that seem to get away from us. With a little planning and imagination we can make the most of both.

BLOCKING INTERRUPTIONS AND DISTRACTIONS

As mentioned earlier, one key to creative success is to be able to carve out large blocks of uninterrupted time. This allows you to concentrate your efforts on the most important goals with the high payoffs. Yet every day, in numerous ways, all of us are subjected to numerous distractions and interruptions. Learning to block and minimize these costly time wasters is a must if you're going to successfully manage your time. Here are some strategies and ideas for dealing with some of the more common ones.

Is It Urgent or Is It Important?

Is your life governed by the tyranny of the urgent? If so, you're in the majority. When Dwight Eisenhower became President he tried to arrange his work so that only those items that were truly urgent and important were called to his attention. However, he quickly discovered that the two seldom went together. The really important items were seldom urgent and the most urgent matters were seldom important. The same principle almost always applies to our daily living. Planning, organizing and concerted action toward long-range goals has no sense of urgency but it's terribly important. However, most of the urgent happenings in our lives are rarely important. What has a greater sense of urgency than the ringing of a telephone, a knock on the door or rushing to a meeting. Yet these are almost always relatively unimportant. Most major crises don't happen without some previous warning.

Dave is a middle-level corporate executive who allows himself to be ruled by urgency. Instead of tackling his tasks in order of importance, he insists on doing his job in a first-come-first-serve manner. This means that all telephone calls are taken as they come and all correspondence (no matter how trivial) is answered immediately. Realizing the importance of good communication, his door is always open for anyone who wants to drop in and pass the time. The result is that Dave doesn't have much time for planning his work or doing the most important tasks. Worse yet, he's forever in hot water with his boss for failing to turn in reports on time. "There's only so much time and I've got too many things to do," he explains. Because he insists on responding to each task with a sense of urgency, many important tasks go neglected and ignored. The result is that he lives from one crisis to another.

As you attempt to manage your time, make a conscious attempt to separate the important from the urgent and work on the important. By putting yourself at the mercy of urgency, you're inviting a life of firefighting, frustration and fatigue.

The Power of Positive "NO-manship"

One almost universal problem of people who have trouble managing time is overcommitment. We live in an age of great expectations and unparalleled opportunity. And too many of us fall into the trap of trying to do it all. No one can. Try to be all things to all people and you'll be nobody to everybody. Don't scatter your efforts like buckshot. Concentrate them and be a big gun. This means saying yes to a few opportunities and no to most. As Lin Yutang pointed out: "Besides the noble art of getting things done, there is the noble art of leaving things undone. The wisdom of life consists in the elimination of nonessentials."

Some years back I compiled "LeBoeuf's Not-to-Do List." It's a simple, concise guide to weeding out the nonessentials that can waste your time. I've found it immensely useful and I hope you will too. Here is the list of things better left undone:

1. All low-priority items—unless the high-priority items have been completed.

2. Any task whose completion is of little or no consequence. When you have something to do, ask yourself the worst thing that could happen if you don't do it. If the answer isn't too bad, then don't do it.

3. Anything you can give to someone else to do. Monta Crane wrote, "There are three ways to get something done: do it yourself, hire someone or forbid your kids to do it." Be smart and choose one of the latter options.

4. Anything just to please others because you fear the condemnation or you want to put them in your debt.

5. Thoughtless or inappropriate requests for your time or effort.

6. Anything others should be doing for themselves.

If you ever get the feeling that you're spinning your wheels, remember the not-to-do list. It may point the way to defining your problem.

The greatest problem that most of us have is simply having the courage to say no. "It makes me feel guilty," is the remark I hear most. This usually stems from the false assumption that someone else's time is more important than yours. Mustering the courage to say no to the unessentials is tough but necessary if you want to master the clock. You will increase your proficiency with practice and the following guidelines will help you:

1. Say no rapidly before people can anticipate that you may say yes. Answers such as "I don't know" or "Let me think about it" only raise false hopes. A delayed no only increases the chances of animosity.

2. Realize that you have the right to say no. You don't have to offer a reason every time you turn down someone's request.

3. Offer your refusals politely and pleasantly. There's no need to be defensive—it's your right to say no.

4. Offer a counterproposal if you think it's appropriate. "I can't keep your children this weekend because we're having guests. However, I'll be happy to do it next weekend." Such an approach softens your refusal.

Minimizing Drop-in Visits and Telephone Calls

These are the two greatest interruptions for most of us. They're almost always unplanned, and if you don't take steps to manage them, visitors and telephone callers can really cut your productive time. To make bad matters worse, they can break your concentration and prevent you from really getting absorbed in the important tasks at hand. Keeping a loose schedule is one way to keep these gremlins from upsetting your workday. No matter how much you try to get away from them, some visitors and callers will always get through. Accept that fact and budget time for it.

To minimize time wasted by visitors and telephone calls, begin by determining who your visitors and callers are. Keep a visitor and telephone log for a week. Write down who calls or visits, what they wanted and how much time they took. Usually the 80/20 Rule will apply. You'll probably find that 80 or more percent of your time taken up by interruptions comes from 20 percent or less of your interruptions. Once you know who your interruptors are, you can devise a strategy for dealing with them. My suggestion is that you arrange to meet or telephone those who are necessary interruptors periodically and take steps to shield yourself from the unnecessary ones. The following is a list of ideas that you may find useful for dealing with visitors:

1. Close your door when you're doing work that requires solitude. Open doors, be it at the office or home, invite the person roaming the halls to drop in and socialize. It's important to be accessible but this doesn't mean you have to be continuously on tap whenever someone wants to visit.

2. Remove excess chairs and social amenities from your office or work area. If you're having trouble getting things done and seem to attract visitors, maybe it's because you're inviting them. Are you the one with the coffeepot and the refrigerator in your office? People may come to think of your place as the gathering spot to socialize. If so, get rid of these things and see what happens. If someone complains, volunteer to move the chairs, coffeepot, refrigerator or whatever to their office.

3. If someone wants to see you, go to their place to chat. This gives you control over the time of the visit. When business is over you can then go back to work in your empty office.

4. If you're a boss who is constantly interrupted by subordinates wanting help with problems, try this: Have them write down the problem, list several alternatives and rank them in order of preference before seeing you. This will increase their decision-making ability and also reduce the length of the visit when you do see them.

5. Use body language. If someone walks into your office unexpectedly, stand up. If someone knocks on your door, confer with them in the hall. This will communicate to others that you're tied up and keep them from planting themselves in your office.

6. It also helps to arrange your desk and chair so that you aren't facing the door. People roaming the halls are more likely to drop in if they make eye contact with you. By not facing the door, you prevent this from happening.

7. If you have a secretary or assistant, position the desk where he or she can screen your unexpected visitors. Provide

information that will allow the assistant to handle problems without you.

8. Schedule regular visiting hours and only see visitors at those times, unless there is an emergency.

9. Use coffee breaks, lunch hours or other committed times to meet with necessary visitors. This makes multiple use of time, and important information can be exchanged.

10. If a visitor gets planted in your office, you can control the length of the visit several ways. If you feel the visitor is overstaying, be quiet. Don't contribute to a needless conversation and there won't be one. You can also arrange for someone else to call you or drop in after a certain time and remind you of another appointment. Or you can simply tell the party you have to be somewhere else in ten minutes and bring the visit to a close.

Telephone calls are another matter. It seems ironic but the telephone is one of our greatest potential time-management tools. It gets information rapidly and saves meetings, visits and transportation time. Unfortunately, for most of us, the telephone is one of our greatest time wasters. The cause of the problem? It's simply a lack of self-discipline on the part of the person receiving the calls. Given the choice between concentrating on the work at hand or being interrupted by the mystery of a telephone call, most of us will opt for the latter. Who is it? What do they want? Maybe it's the deal of a lifetime! It rarely is. Most likely it's someone who has nothing better to do. In addition to keeping a telephone log, try these ideas for reducing telephone time:

1. Use the telephone for saving rather than wasting time. Hold conference calls instead of meetings. Telephone in lieu of writing letters and memos when possible. Proper use of the telephone can be a real time and money saver.

2. Establish a period of time each day for placing and receiving calls. Morning is usually the best time. Encourage people to call at those hours. Grouping your outgoing calls will also be helpful.

3. Put a small, three-minute hourglass by your phone. Every time you place or receive a call, see if you can success-

fully complete it in three minutes. Don't rush. Obviously some calls will take much longer and rightly so. Keep a scorecard and see if you can reduce your telephone time each week. Make a game out of it and reward yourself each week you reduce your telephone time.

4. Have your calls screened by an assistant or a telephone-answering machine. Assistants can screen your calls tactfully without making you seem inaccessible. Your assistant can say: "He's rather tied up at the moment. Would you like to have me interrupt him or may I have him call you back?" Most will opt for the call back. Of course, most assistants will probably be able to provide information to callers without interrupting you the majority of the time. Telephone-answering machines are in the price range of almost everyone today. In addition to screening calls, the machine answers your telephone when you can't, and you never miss a call. As a writer, I've found this to be an extremely worthwhile investment. Most models also have an optional attachment that plays back messages to you if you call your machine while away from home or office.

5. Before you place a call, outline the information you wish to convey or receive. This will reduce the chances that you'il forget something and have to call back. Once you're on the phone, set the tone of the conversation at the beginning with "The reason I'm calling is . . ."

6. Once you've transacted business, bring the conversation to a prompt and polite close. If you're having trouble getting rid of a long-winded caller, hang up in the middle of one of your own sentences. It may be impolite to hang up on him but Amy Vanderbilt never said anything about hanging up on yourself! If he has anything important to add, he will call back, and if not he will probably go bother somebody else.

They Can't Interrupt You if They Can't Find You

It's always good to have someplace where you can find solitude when you need it. As was pointed out earlier, creative thought and action frequently require it. Therefore, consider the following possible hideaways as alternatives to escaping interruptions:

1. If you work for a company, see if they have rooms set aside for people who need solitude to complete their work.

2. Libraries can be great places to hide out. Many of them have soundproof carrels you can rent.

3. You can have an arrangement with someone else where you agree to swap offices. You can work in his office undisturbed and he can work in yours.

4. Rent a hotel or motel room—the farther away, the better.

5. If you need lengthy periods of solitude, consider renting an apartment. I know several authors who have tried this with excellent results.

6. You can always use your car for temporary hibernation. Drive to a secluded spot and do your working or thinking in your car.

When you hibernate be sure to let your whereabouts be known to only those who need to reach you in case of emergency. Otherwise you'll run the risk of being interrupted at your hideaway.

Manage Trivia by Batching It

Paying bills, running errands, shopping, housework, yard work, making minor repairs, correspondence, reading and making telephone calls are all examples of necessary minor tasks that all of us are faced with in our daily lives. One sure way to waste time is to tackle them in a random fashion. To keep trivia from disrupting your day, batch it. Collect a number of minor tasks and then have a trivia session to take care of them. Napoleon used this with great results. He opened his mail only once every three weeks! It not only saved him time each day, but by the time three weeks had passed many of the problems had been resolved without his help. The energy crisis is fast teaching us to batch our errands. Take the same approach to paying bills, writing letters and the like.

A FINAL WORD ABOUT THE BIG TIME CONSUMERS

The average American spends almost half of his time engaging in two activities, sleeping and watching television. We spend approximately a third of our life sleeping and one fourth of our waking hours glued to the one-eyed monster. Can we salvage any time here? In the former case, perhaps. In the latter case, most definitely.

In the case of sleep, your goal is to be able to get the minimum amount of sleep and still feel rested and energetic. To determine that amount, begin by setting your alarm fifteen minutes earlier than you currently do. Do this for one week and see how you feel at the end of a week. If you feel rested, drop it another fifteen minutes the following week and continue doing this each week until you begin to feel tired. Then move the alarm up fifteen minutes. That should be close to your optimum level of sleep. I once averaged nine hours sleep per day but through that exercise I successfully reduced my sleep time to seven hours with no feelings of fatigue.

That adds up to an extra sixty hours per month or seven hundred thirty hours in a year. And that's a lot of time! For example, it took me a total of about three hundred hours to write this book.

Groucho Marx once remarked, "I find television very educating. Every time somebody turns on the set I go into the other room and read a book." If Groucho lived in a typical household, he must have been well read. Americans spend an average twenty-seven hours and nineteen minutes per week viewing what Frank Lloyd Wright called chewing gum for the eyes. It isn't appropriate for me to tell you how much television viewing is right for you. It's your time, your life and your decision. However, for many of us a great amount of television time is a gigantic waste.

If you feel that you're spending too much time in front of the tube, put yourself on a television diet. First determine how many hours you feel you should be watching and plan ahead. Make a list of your favorite programs and rank them in order of importance. Once again you'll find the 80/20 Rule applies and that 80 percent of your viewing pleasure comes from 20 percent or less of your viewing time. Then resolve to watch only as many hours as you have planned. If you have trouble disciplining yourself, put a timer on your television and program it to turn off the set when your favorite show is over. Don't make drastic cuts in viewing time. Try reducing it fifteen minutes each week until you have it to a level you feel is more in keeping with good use of your time.

A lot of viewing time is wasted with commercials that are of absolutely no interest to you. Have some trivial or routine tasks at hand to work on when the commercials come on. In this regard, it helps to have a remote control that allows you to turn off the sound during commercials.

Video recorders can also help reduce television time. You can program them to record several programs and play them back at your leisure. This allows you to make use of your prime time for doing important tasks and keeps your favorite shows from interrupting something important you may be working on.

When it comes to creative success, other than your imagination, there is nothing more important than knowing how to manage your time. Time is life itself and as Fred Allen pointed out: "You only live once. But if you work it right, once is enough."

11

The Word Is ACTION

"Hoping to goodness is not theologically sound!"

—Linus

ACCORDING TO JOHN NEWBERN, people can be divided into three groups: those who make things happen, those who watch things happen, and those who wonder what happened. Although this may be an artificial and overly simplistic attempt at stereotyping, it does make a significant point. To be an imagineer means being a person of action. Imagination is wonderful stuff but it simply isn't enough. It takes action, and plenty of it, to turn your ideas into successful realities.

A good case can be made that action (or the lack of it) is the weak link in the imagineering process. Every year numerous patents are taken out on ideas that never get to the marketplace. Book publishers frequently negotiate contracts for books that never come to pass. It seems that some authors never get around to writing. Start paying attention to daily conversations and you'll soon discover that people are literally full of good ideas for better living. You'll hear ideas for their dream home, schemes to make lots of money, how they plan to get a better job and on, and on, and on. Yet how many of these great ideas become realities? Very, very few. If only one percent of the great ideas in this world ever became realities, the progress of mankind would increase at least a hundredfold.

What's the problem? In a nutshell, it's that people usually don't follow through. If you've ever learned to swing a baseball bat, a golf club or kick a football, you know the importance of following through. I saw a television program recently that featured a five-year-old billiards champion.

195

When asked to explain his technique as a pool shooter, he replied, "I don't poke, I stroke." At only five years of age, he knew the importance of following through. If he can transfer that idea from the green-felted table to the rest of his life, he will be in better shape than most of us. Unfortunately, most of us spend our lives poking at ideas rather than following through and turning them into realities.

How do you solve the follow-through problem? I recommend a three-point plan of attack. First, you must understand and conquer procrastination, which probably prevents us from following through more than anything else. Second, you master the art of creating enthusiasm that will motivate you and keep your spirits high. Finally, you must cultivate the habit of being intelligently persistent when the situation calls for it. No doubt, this is a large order, but following through is a large problem. Let's tackle those solutions one at a time.

THE PUT-OFF GAME

Everyone is a procrastinator. Everyone. Overcoming the inertia of not doing and pushing ourselves to pursue important goals is a challenge that each of us faces every day. Indeed, many of us are at our most creative when it comes to thinking up reasons to delay tackling major projects. Does this sound like you? You've set aside a large block of time to devote to turning that dream of yours into reality. There are no interruptions or distractions. Everything is ideal. And then just as you're about to begin . . .

1. You're suddenly overwhelmed by fatigue. Better take a nap first. Or . . .

2. You're famished. So you go make a sandwich or consume several candy bars. Or . . .

3. You remember that you have to call your brother-in-law to tell him that you can't go fishing Saturday. So you pick up the phone and call him. Or . . .

4. You realize it's time for your favorite TV program or the news is coming on. The international situation has you wor-

ried and you won't be able to think straight unless you hear the news. Or . . .

5. _____

_____

_____

(Use this space to fill in your own favorite reason for putting off.)

The ability of the human imagination approaches its peak when coming up with reasons for procrastinating. As an anonymous philosopher put it, "We are all manufacturers—some make good, others make trouble and still others make excuses."

Why Do We Play It?

We play the put-off game with ourselves for several reasons. The greatest reason for putting off major tasks is that it masks our own fears of failure. Either the task looks so large at the outset that we feel sure we will never finish it, or if we do finish it it won't be a satisfactory job. Therefore, we come up with all sorts of ideas for not starting.

Bill dreams of being an attorney. He has an undergraduate degree, good entrance-exam scores and has been admitted to law school for the coming year. He has a full-time job that bores him and he would like nothing better than to be an attorney. He worked his way through college part-time in a law office and knows what the business is about. But as the school year approaches, Bill has second thoughts. He enjoys the income of a full-time job, and law school is three grueling years of work without pay. "Of course, I could go to night school, but that would take forever," he thinks to himself. "Besides, who feels like studying and listening to professors ramble on after working all day? Worse yet, even if I do make all these sacrifices and graduate, I still might fail the bar exam. All would be for naught." Thus, Bill successfully talks himself into passing up law school. "Maybe next year I'll give it a try," he thinks. Fat chance. Bill stays in a job that bores him and his goals go down the drain. Bill has been duped into procrastinating by his own fears of failure.

Unpleasant tasks are another major source of delay. Everything you want in life has a price (in terms of money, time or effort) attached to it. The price frequently consists of unpleasant tasks to perform. Executives have to fire people, resolve conflicts and be bearers of bad news. Fighters have to do road work. Students have to do homework. The story goes that a famous violinist was stopped on the street in New York by a tourist and asked, "How do you get to Carnegie Hall?" He replied, "Practice!" If you want to roll the dice, you have to be willing to pay the price. Given the option of doing something pleasant or unpleasant, most of us will do the former. Thus we tend to put off important, unpleasant tasks and fill up our present moments with trivia which makes us feel like we're accomplishing something.

Procrastination is a great cop-out for a poor effort. "I just couldn't get around to it until the last minute" is the common story of the procrastinator. One favorite procrastination excuse is to tell yourself that you work best under pressure. This rationalization gives you the liberty of waiting until the last minute to begin a crash program. Unfortunately, most crash programs end up exactly like they're named. Murphy loves to play havoc with rush jobs. If you can't find the time to do it right the first time, where will you find the time to do it again?

Procrastination also leads to all sorts of real and imagined excuses for no effort at all. It never ceases to amaze me how many college students report their grandparents dying the night before an exam. It's a medical phenomenon. I once gave an exam and had four grandparent deaths reported in one day. Some weeks later, I had the pleasure of meeting one of the "deceased" grandparents. She informed me that reports of her death were greatly exaggerated.

Procrastination gives you the luxury of becoming a critic, which takes a whole lot less effort and self-examination than striving to reach your goals. Most critics are little more than frustrated doers.

Perfectionism leads to procrastination. The only way to avoid mistakes is to avoid action. Compulsive perfectionists love to play the put-off game.

Hoping a major problem will solve itself is another cause of delay or inaction. Sometimes this works, but more often than not problems create worse problems if action isn't taken to solve them. This leaves you burdened with worse problems than you originally had plus any new ones that come up in the meantime. All of which lead to unnecessary frustration and fatigue.

People frequently put things off in order to get someone else to do the work. There's nothing inherently wrong with delegating, but why play games? Hire or request someone to do the job and get it done.

Improper goals can lead to procrastination. Is this goal still important or necessary? Goals without deadlines tend to get achieved much later or never achieved.

People who overcommit themselves are usually chronic procrastinators. Saying yes to everything decreases the chances of completing the important things.

Unrealistic, tight schedules can cause procrastination. Expecting too much of yourself can cause unnecessary bottlenecks and delays. So can a lack of information.

Procrastination is a great vehicle for resisting change. It gives you license to stay in a rut, not make decisions, waste your life and blame your misfortunes on everyone else. In short, delay leads to decay.

Action Is the Cure for Inaction

There is practically no limit to what some of us will go to to be able to indulge ourselves in the "luxury" of doing nothing. Yet all too often those who get their way find that a permanent vacation is the worst job in the world. The inaction caused by procrastinating puts you under a useless strain of guilt, pressure, feelings of uselessness and subsequent frustration and fatigue. Ironically, putting things off is very hard work. If you really want to avoid a useless strain, recognize the futility of the procrastination habit and resolve to banish it from your life.

The key to conquering procrastination is to make a start on whatever it is that you're avoiding. Once you're in motion, the momentum of getting started will tend to keep you moving. The following are some specific techniques that you can use to create the necessary momentum to get you started:

1. Meet procrastination head on. Self-discipline is at the core of conquering procrastination, and you don't acquire self-discipline by sweeping problems under the rug. Decide what it is that you're putting off that stands between you and your dreams. Write it down. Why are you procrastinating? Is it overwhelming? Unpleasant? Time consuming? Pin down the problem and you'll be better able to devise a strategy for ending the delay.

2. Divide and conquer. As I pointed out in Chapter Nine, it's easy to get overwhelmed by large tasks and confuse them with situational hurdles when, in fact, it's just procrastination. Break those large tasks into small ones, complete with deadlines, and tackle them one at a time.

3. Don't allow yourself to make excuses for putting off those things that are most important to you. In the final analysis, excuses don't count and results do. If you give yourself the liberty of making excuses, you'll always be able to come up with an ample supply. Take your most important task and get started on it—now.

4. If you catch yourself procrastinating, give yourself a pep talk. Lay it on the line and goad yourself into action. I used that technique to tackle the beginning of this book. I had recently returned from New York, where I had spoken with my agents about the idea for a book on creativity. They were enthusiastic and asked me to send them a book outline in one month. This meant I had to go home and get to work immediately, if not sooner. As I sat at my desk trying to generate ideas, I started coming up empty handed. I couldn't think of any ideas. That's when I realized I was procrastinating and not producing. "Some writer you are!" I thought to myself. "You want to write on creativity and you can't even come up with enough ideas for a lousy book. This is absurd and inexcusable. You are going to write this book. It may be the worst book ever written. It may sell only thirty-eight copies. But it's gonna get written." I pictured myself appearing in Ripley's "Believe It or Not." "Michael LeBoeuf set out to write a book about creating new ideas and turning them into realities. However, the book was never written due to a lack of ideas." With that, I settled down and started generating ideas, and the outline was finished with time to spare.

5. Reserve a small amount of time to work on an unpleas-

ant task. Schedule fifteen minutes or a half-hour next week to devote to cleaning out the garage or straightening a closet. Resolve to work on the task and quit when your time is up. If the task can't be handled piecemeal, just do it and let it be done. By avoiding the unpleasant task you only compound future problems.

6. Do a start-up task. Sometimes physical action can provide the spunk to get you in the mood to tackle a major task. Do you want to paint a landscape? Go purchase the necessary paints and supplies—now. The physical activity and financial commitment can provide the momentum to get you going.

7. Capitalize on your moods. You may not be in the mood to tackle the proposal for the new advertising campaign but do you feel like gathering some of the background data and information? Become sensitive to your moods and do things when you're hot to do them.

8. Think of the most important goal or dream that you keep putting off pursuing. Then take a sheet of paper and list all the advantages of tackling the task on one side of the page and all the disadvantages of not tackling the task on the other side. The advantages of action will usually outweigh the disadvantages of inaction manyfold. Seeing this on paper can create the incentive to get you moving.

9. Make a wager or commitment. Take your greatest creative goal and tell someone you will reach it by a particular date or, better yet, bet them. Making a commitment to other people will give you additional motivation to get moving and turn that idea into a reality. If you bet with someone, be sure there's an incentive for reaching your goal and a penalty for falling short.

10. Give yourself a deadline and a reward. Promise yourself that you'll complete that project you have been delaying by a certain date and then choose a fitting reward for yourself in the event you succeed. This is a fun way to conquer procrastination and it keeps life interesting. Keep the size of the reward commensurate with the project. For major projects, such as going back to school to get an advanced degree, promise yourself something really nice like a new car, vacation or whatever seems appropriate. Rewards can also provide the incentive for doing smaller tasks too. If you can use the reward system, be honest with yourself. Don't give yourself the

reward if you don't complete the job and be sure to reward yourself if you do complete the job.

11. Practice doing nothing. When you find yourself avoiding something important, don't fill up the time with trivia. Instead go sit in a chair and do absolutely nothing. Don't watch television, or read or anything. Do nothing. Pretty soon you'll come to realize what a drag it is. When you can't take it any longer, get up and start on that project you've been putting off—now.

12. Answer this question each day: "What is the greatest problem facing me and what am I going to do about it today?" Once you have an answer, get to work on the problem—now. Another question you can answer is "What's the best use of my time and energy right now?" Focusing on the answers to those questions will help keep procrastination from standing between you and your dreams.

FAN THE FIRES OF ENTHUSIASM

Enthusiasm is a crucial ingredient of creative living. It's enthusiasm that sparks imagination. It's enthusiasm that transforms a boring, tired person into a beautiful creative one. Enthusiasm is the difference between relishing your career and going through the motions of doing a job. Indeed, one can make a good case that a life without enthusiasm is hardly one worth living.

According to *The Catholic Layman*, "Every man is enthusiastic at times. One man has enthusiasm for thirty minutes—another has it for thirty days—but it is the man who has it for thirty years who makes a success in life." Yet every day all of us meet people of unquestionable ability who appear to be sleepwalking through life. If you feel you're one of those people, I have good news. You don't have to be that way. You can consciously choose to be enthusiastic. Enthusiasm is an attitude and one that has to be fed, nurtured and cultivated in order to keep it functioning. It's the electricity of the soul, and you can't expect the batteries to run forever without recharging them. Enthusiasm has to be nourished with new actions, new aspirations, new efforts and new vision. It's your problem if your enthusiasm is on the decline and it's your job to get it back. If you want to turn hours into minutes, labor into pleasant tasks and dreams into realities you must continually renew your enthusiasm. The following ideas, if diligently applied, will equip you with an ample supply of this most precious intangible. They have worked for others and they can work for you too.

Make a Commitment

It takes courage to be enthusiastic about your dreams because real enthusiasm is an indicator of commitment. The more you believe in a dream and give yourself to it, the more enthusiastic you will automatically become. Enthusiasm is the product of a person's commitment to a goal. This is why it's so terribly important to set and pursue goals that *you* want to achieve and sincerely believe in. As Charles Buxton put it: "Experience shows that success is due less to ability than to zeal. The winner is he who gives himself to his work, body and soul."

Get More Information

Let's suppose you have an idea, task or goal that doesn't excite you. However, you wish you were excited about it. In this case, resolve to learn more about the topic. The things that interest us least are usually the things that we know least about. As you learn more about a subject, your interest and enthusiasm usually will tend to increase. I've seen people who hated football become rabid fans after learning that there's a lot more to the game than bodies crashing into each other. I've seen people who despised opera become opera buffs after discovering that it's a whole lot more than screaming women. Before writing a book, I thought that publishing was a rather dull business. However, in the process of trying to learn more about the business I discovered that the publishing world is a fascinating, complex and exciting one. It's anything but dull. Only my ignorance had led me to believe it was. So it is with most things in life. More often than not, a lack of interest is due to a lack of information or understanding. Find those things you want to get excited about and learn all you can about them. With the knowledge will come enthusiasm.

Related to this is the terribly important need to communicate with enthusiasm. This is particularly necessary when the realization of your dreams involves a team effort. Put life into your expression. Don't just paste on a smile. Smile with your eyes and your entire face. Speak and shake hands with vitality. Exchange pleasantries with meaning. Most people say such things as "good morning," "thank you" and "congratulations" with the sterile monotone of a talking robot. Put your feelings into your words and say them with vitality. Be a bearer of good news. We all like to be around cheerful people who radiate a positive vitality for life. Their buoyancy is contagious and stimulates creative thought and action. Why not be one of them? You can if you choose to.

Make Something Happen

Many of us lack enthusiasm because we sit around waiting for it to magically descend upon us. Good luck, but don't bet on it happening. If you wake up most days feeling unenthusiastic it's probably because you aren't expecting anything exciting to happen. Expectation about what you feel the future holds is a major factor in determining how enthusiastic you will be. Therefore, to create your own enthusiasm, create your own excitement. Go back and look over your goals and the creativity exercises. Find something to sink your teeth into. Choose a project whose long-range potential would be immensely rewarding to your inner fulfillment and go after it starting today. Practice expecting the best from yourself and the situation. Positive and great expectations have a way of bringing out the best in all of us. And despite the final outcome, isn't that all we can give? Expect the best and make something happen. If you practice this, you'll never find yourself short of enthusiasm.

Look for the Good in Every Situation

It's easy to be enthusiastic and motivated when everything is going well. Success takes care of itself, and as Joe Namath put it, "When you win, nothing hurts." It's the ability to maintain enthusiasm in the face of misfortune and adversity that often spells the difference between success and failure. Adversity and setbacks are a part of everyone's life. However, it doesn't necessarily follow that adversity must decrease your enthusiasm.

To maintain enthusiasm in the face of adversity, you must realize that life, above all, is a state of mind—an attitude. What happens to you isn't nearly so important as what you think about what happens to you. Keep your sense of perspective and learn something from everything you experience, no matter how unpleasant. Then, resolve to use what you've learned to make the future better for you and yours. The late Senator Hubert Humphrey provides an excellent example. In 1968 he barely lost the presidential election after trailing in the polls by a wide margin some months earlier. It was one of his toughest battles and a heartbreaking loss. However, even in this defeat he managed to keep his enthusiasm. Some years later he wrote:

> To come as close as we finally did to winning the highest office in this land and then to lose was hard. But in writing my concession speech, I told myself, "This has to be done right because it is the *opening* speech of your next campaign!" I was already looking ahead.

Like all politicians, Hubert Humphrey had his critics and detractors, but no one ever doubted his abundant supply of enthusiasm. No doubt, he learned the value of such a practice during the dark days of the Depression about which he wrote:

> My family lost a lot, especially during the Depression. One of my saddest memories is of my mother crying and my dad with tears in his eyes because they had to

sell our home to pay the bills. But in life it isn't what you've lost, it's what you've got left that counts. We had a lot left. We had ourselves, our family, our store. It was only a question of time before things would get better. The important thing was who would be the survivors. Who had the will to hang on for a better day.

I think the biggest mistake people make is giving up. Adversity is an experience, not a final act. Some people look upon any setback as the end. They're always looking for the benediction rather than the invocation. Most of us have enough problems so that almost any day we could fold up and say, "I've had it." But you can't quit. That isn't the way our country was built.*

Which leads us to our third and final ingredient for successfully following through:

CULTIVATE THE HABIT OF INTELLIGENT PERSISTENCE

A never-give-up attitude is essential for any kind of major success, and this is particularly true for creative success. As M. H. Alderson remarked, "If at first you don't succeed, you are running about average." All of us have heard numerous success stories of the individual who was willing to try one more time and succeeded when the overwhelming temptation was to throw in the towel. The author submits her manuscript to one more publisher after numerous rejections and it becomes a best seller. The fighter fights one more round when he's exhausted and lands a knockout punch. The performer goes to one more audition and becomes a superstar. Someone goes to one more job interview and launches a successful career. The list is endless.

Make no mistake about it. Perseverance is essential. But it isn't enough. Blind perseverance is for fools. Following

*Hubert Humphrey, "You Can't Quit," *Reader's Digest,* vol. 3, no. 664 (August 1977), pp. 58–59.

through successfully requires intelligent persistence. This means combining a never-give-up attitude with some practical techniques that will help you to reach your goals more efficiently and effectively.

You Must Believe It's Possible

No one knows what any of us is capable of achieving. However, one thing we do know is that we aren't capable of achieving that which we believe is impossible. Once you're convinced that you are fighting a losing battle, a losing battle is what it becomes, and your follow-through will tend to suffer. Don't fall into this trap. Ask yourself: Is it possible? If so, proceed at full speed. This is why it's vitally important to set goals that you believe are attainable.

Keep the Final Goal in Mind

As you pursue your dreams, keep that ultimate goal in mind and stress the benefits that you will realize from achieving it. Make a list of those benefits and put them where you can see them. Refer to them when you need the motivation to keep going. One couple I know put up the architectural plans for their dream home on the wall of their apartment. This constantly reminded them to keep saving and sacrificing to make that ultimate dream a reality. Constantly remind yourself of the benefits of achieving your goals.

Experiment and Adapt

Thomas Edison was a very persistent imagineer. However, he always was trying new things in an attempt to get better results. This is a technique that all of us can profit from. As you attempt to turn your ideas into realities, don't be afraid to try new ways to get better results. And use the information from these results to lead you to greater successes. This is really nothing more than an application of the feedback principle which you may be familiar with. In this case we can illustrate it with the following simple diagram:

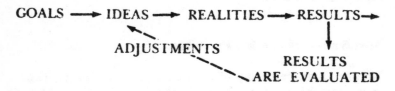

There are numerous examples where this can be applied. Businesses experiment with new products and services and change on the basis of the results they get. Artists, writers and performers must experiment continually with new approaches to getting their message across. Football teams try various plays and defenses in the first half and on the basis of their results adjust in the second half. The major point is to keep probing and searching for better ways to achieve your goals as you pursue them.

Don't Burn Yourself Out

One sure way to turn creative absorption into drudgery is to never get away from the task. Workaholism can be hazardous to your health and your creative ability. When you feel yourself losing your edge for performing a task, back off and take a break. If you find yourself blocked from solving a problem, make a tactical retreat. Pushing ahead will only lead to confusion and frustration. Rest your mind by putting the problem aside. Perhaps you need more information or time for incubation.

Another tactic to prevent following through from becoming drudgery is plan your work so that it will appear enjoyable and productive when you start back. The following techniques can help:

1. Try to end your work on a point of satisfaction or achievement. If you do this, you will tend to think of the job as gratifying and be more eager to return to it.

2. If you quit at a point where you are stalled, write the

problem down. Thinking on paper tends to clarify ideas and increases the chances of finding a solution.

3. Have a logical starting point planned for when you return to the task. This will reduce your start-up time and prevent you from feeling like you're spinning your wheels.

Refuse to Be Beaten

Finally, intelligent persistence requires a healthy dose of hard-headed perseverance. There's absolutely no substitute for the willingness to keep going and push yourself to give that extra effort. As Charles Kettering put it: "Keep going and the chances are you will stumble on something, perhaps when you are least expecting it. I never heard of anyone stumbling on something sitting down." More than anything else, genius is the power of making continual efforts. You only fail when you cease to try and the only real defeat is that which comes from within. Refuse to be beaten. Don't look back. The great fighter James J. Corbett said it best:

> Fight one more round. When your feet are so tired that you have to shuffle back to the center of the ring, fight one more round. When your arms are so tired that you can hardly lift your hands to come on guard, fight one more round. When your nose is bleeding and your eyes are black and you are so tired that you wish your opponent would crack you one in the jaw and put you to sleep, fight one more round—remembering that the man who always fights one more round is never whipped.

Conquering procrastination, maintaining enthusiasm and intelligent persistence are the necessary ingredients of a successful follow-through. And successfully following through is the final phase of imagineering.

12

Creative Absorption, the Real Fun in Life

"The rapture of pursuing is the prize."
—Henry Wadsworth Longfellow

WE HAVE COME full cycle in our journey through the joys, trials and tribulations of imagineering. As you now realize there's a lot more to creativity than simply thinking grandiose thoughts. Creating new ideas and turning your dreams into realities is no easy business. However, it's far from total drudgery and there is one fantastic payoff that we have yet to mention. That payoff has been termed "flow," and for many it's the greatest reward of creative thinking and acting.

You experience flow by becoming creatively absorbed in a dream or a task. Doing the task becomes its own reward. People who become creatively absorbed speak of experiencing an ecstatic joy while involved in the creative process. Work becomes play. Concentration becomes automatic. Time passes infinitely faster. Concern and evaluation of self totally vanishes. The process creates rather than depletes energy. You feel relaxed, in control and at peace and in harmony with the universe.

Psychologists studying creative absorption and the flow experience believe that this is one of man's natural highs. When we lose ourselves to the task of creating, the feelings of joy and ecstasy automatically follow. For some, the greatest joys in life don't come from money, prestige or idleness. They come from experiencing flow as a result of total immersion in what we're doing. As one musical composer put it, "You are in an ecstatic state to such a point that you don't exist."

In one sense, the essence of this book has been to provide

you with practical techniques that will enable you to experience the flow of the creative process. No doubt you can also use these ideas to bring you power, prestige, more money or whatever you choose. However, it's my opinion that the greatest reward you'll reap from being an imagineer is the feeling of inner richness and joy that comes from turning your dreams into realities. In these final pages I would like to summarize the major points that have been presented. This capsule view of key ideas and questions is intended to give you an understanding and overview of the entire imagineering process. You may find it helpful later on as a quick reference.

1. Do you accept the fact that you are creative? You and every other human being of normal ability is endowed with a large amount of untapped creative potential. Due to experiences, education and background, most of us have been taught to suppress rather than develop our imaginations. Recognize and be aware of all the numerous myths and excuses that can inhibit your creative growth and resolve to throw off those mental shackles. This is a prerequisite for creative success. Removing the creativity myths from your life will require an open mind and changing preconceived values. But your only alternative is to overshadow creativity with ignorance. As Walter Kelly put it, "The man who never alters his opinions is like standing water and breeds reptiles of the mind."

2. Do you have a well-thought-out set of goals and priorities? Goals serve as the foundation for personal growth, fulfillment and direction and enable you to channel your time and energy. The world makes way for those who know what they want and have the courage to pursue it. Set specific, written goals that you feel are challenging but attainable. Resolve to pursue the most important ones each day, but always consider your goals flexible and subject to revision or change. As you grow this will no doubt become necessary. Always keep your ultimate goals in mind to prevent you from falling into the activity trap. The words of Albert Einstein are truer today than ever: "Perfection of means and confusion of ends seem to characterize our age." Keep the 80/20 Rule in mind and concentrate on pursuing the most important goals. Eighty percent of your achievement can be found by meeting 20 percent or less of your goals.

3. As you strive to generate new ideas, accept the fact that the heart of all new ideas lies in the borrowing, adding, combining or modifying of old ones. As Mark Twain put it, "Adam was the only man who, when he said a good thing, knew that nobody had said it before him." Remember that the act of generating new ideas goes through a predictable cycle of steps that will occur over varying periods of time. The stages of first insight, preparation, incubation, illumination and verification are all necessary for the generation of good, new ideas.

4. Have you created a climate for yourself that is conducive to creativity? Give yourself plenty of incentive for generating ideas and challenge yourself to meet deadlines for generating ideas. You must, above all, refrain from thinking up and judging simultaneously. First think up, then judge your ideas. Generate new ideas in the spirit of humor and playfulness. This will keep the flow of ideas coming. Think of it as fun even though the results of your work may be very serious. As you create new ideas, focus on only one thing at a time. Be alert for personal touches or rituals that help you generate new ideas and use them.

5. Are you developing and exercising your idea-producing capacity? The drive to produce new ideas is the single largest determining factor in how creative you will become. There are numerous ways to exercise your imagination, such as experience, reading, hobbies, writing, crafts and the like. Choose those that appeal most to you and work on improving your dream machine.

6. New ideas can also be mechanically induced. Checklists, forced relationships, attribute listing and morphological approaches can enable us to turn out numerous new ideas at will.

7. Are you capitalizing on your hunches? Be alert for any hunches you feel and evaluate them as potentially good ideas. As Frank Capra put it, "A hunch is creativity trying to tell you something."

8. Are you documenting your ideas as you generate them? Thoughts are fleeting and new ideas will rapidly vanish from your memory unless you record them. Always have a pencil and paper or a tape recording nearby. Get yourself an idea

bank and start accumulating your thoughts. You may soon acquire a very profitable collection.

9. Have you set aside a definite time and place for generating ideas? All of us are creatures of habit and if you consciously choose a time and place for idea generating, new ideas will come with regularity as you cultivate the habit.

10. Do you have an idea team for thinking up? People interacting in groups can generate numerous ideas that they wouldn't have thought of alone. However, it's important to realize that team creativity should be a supplement to, rather than a substitute for, individual creativity. Every idea is the product of a single brain. When thinking up in groups, be sure to refrain from judging ideas until after the members of the group have completed generating ideas. Promote a spirit of playfulness and encourage people to build on each other's ideas.

11. Do you use the question technique to generate new ideas and solutions to problems? First, isolate the subject or problem you want to think about and then ask a series of questions about each step of the subject or problem. Can it be done better? More cheaply? Can something else be adapted? Be alert to the numerous questions available for ideation and use them when the need arises. As Einstein put it, "The important thing is to not stop questioning."

12. Do you evaluate your ideas before committing yourself to them? As Joseph Joubert remarked, "He who has imagination without learning has wings but no feet." No one really has a foolproof method for telling if an idea is a good one. However, there are several sets of criteria that will remove many of the bad ones. Remember that the vast majority of ideas will not pass the criteria for evaluating them. Choose only those with the highest probability of success. If an idea seems to measure up as a good one, test it on a small scale, if possible.

13. Do you take a positive approach to the problems you face? A peaceful mind is one that will foster creative thought and action. Strive to rid yourself of negative emotions that can jam your creative machinery. Build your creative self-image by attempting to become innovative and by opening your mind to new alternatives to living and problem solving. Remember

these two things about your creative ability: 1) it's unknown and 2) it's underestimated.

14. As you turn your dreams into realities, do you strive to get people working with you rather than against you? No one ever achieves anything totally by himself. As Walt Disney put it, "You can dream, design and build the most wonderful place in the world, but it requires people to make the dream a reality." In trying to innovate, be ready to encounter resistance to change and a healthy amount of criticism: Work at skillfully overcoming the former through openness, two-way communication and allowing people to participate in the change. As for the critics, who needs them? If you have evaluated your ideas thoroughly and believe strongly in them, the critics can offer you little or nothing of substantial value. Ignore them and seek evaluation from those whose judgment you trust. As Mignon McLaughlin said: "Nobody wants constructive criticism. It's all we can do to put up with constructive praise."

15. Building a winning team begins with the best, goal-oriented, positive-thinking people you can get your hands on. Strive to hire or recruit people who are smarter than you are. It isn't what people cost that counts. It's what they're worth. Once you have a good team—delegate, delegate, delegate. Good people need latitude to do a quality job. Be lavish in your praise and quick to recognize excellence. There's no limit to what can be done if you don't insist on getting the credit.

16. Are you building a network of contacts who can help you realize your dreams? Talk to friends, relatives and associates who may be able to help you or refer you to someone who can. Seek out those people and organizations that may find your idea useful and call or, better yet, go see them in person. The more contacts you are able to establish, the greater the chances of finding one that will be mutually beneficial.

17. Are you patient? There is almost no limit to what can be accomplished if you give things time to develop. Realize that we live in an essentially impatient society of instant need gratification. Don't throw up your hands and abandon your dreams too soon. As W. B. Prescott wrote, "In any contest between power and patience, bet on patience."

18. Are you working at improving your luck? It's possible.

Good luck is opportunity meeting preparation. Be ready to make the most of opportunities by preparing beforehand. You must be willing to take calculated risks but always have an alternate route to bail you out if things go bad. Limit your losses by getting out of bad situations before they become worse. One reason lucky people are lucky is because they never rely on the fickleness of fate to save them.

19. Are you letting a lack of money stand between you and your dreams? Don't. Good ideas will attract money and there are plenty of people who are willing to help if you seek them out. What you perceive as a money problem is nothing more than a shortage of ideas for raising money. You can raise money by borrowing, by selling tangible assets and through various fund-raising activities. Flex your creative muscles and you'll come up with plenty of ways to raise the money you need.

20. Don't allow inexperience to stop you either. It's one thing none of us are born with. Don't worry about doing a poor job. If you're trying something new, give yourself the luxury of being bad. Don't compete with anyone but yourself and keep trying to improve. Mistakes are part of the cost of learning. Volunteer to work for someone in exchange for experience. Learn all you can about what you want to do. Sooner or later the inexperience hurdle will vanish.

21. Are you managing your time or is it managing you? As Ben Hecht noted, "Time is like a circus, always packing up and moving away." Successful imagineers know how to use their time to get things done. They move steadily toward their goals at a comfortable but effective pace. They realize that one of the problems of hurry is that it takes such a long time. Periodically keep a time log to see if you are spending your time on those things that are truly important to you. Make a daily to-do list and be sure to schedule a quiet time for yourself each day. Try to perform your most important tasks during prime time. Schedule loosely and be sure to leave plenty of time for you. Be prepared to make the most of already committed time. Knowing how to manage time is a major key to making things happen. Take heed of what Ben Franklin wrote two hundred years ago: "Does thou love life? Then do not squander time, for that's the stuff life is made of."

22. Have you reserved large blocks of uninterrupted time

to pursue your dreams? Creative thought and action requires that you spend large amounts of time concentrating on the most important goals in your life. Distinguish between the urgent and the important. Learn to say no and avoid overcommitment. Take steps to shield yourself from distracting interruptions. Handle trivia in batches and cut down on your television time. Large creative successes demand that you do these things.

23. Are you making a concerted effort to conquer procrastination? It's a never-ending battle that all of us must fight every day. Realize that there are numerous irrational reasons for which all of us tend to put things off and get those demons out of your life. Chop up overwhelming tasks into small tasks. Give yourself a deadline and a reward for achieving your goals. Realize that the hardest part is getting started and resolve to rid yourself of this useless, burdensome habit. As Eugene Ware remarked, "All glory comes from daring to begin."

24. Never underestimate the power of enthusiasm. As H. W. Arnold put it, "Let a man lose everything in the world but his enthusiasm and he will come through again to success." Enthusiasm is a major ingredient of creative success, and each individual must maintain and build his own ample supply. You gain enthusiasm for a task by committing yourself to it and digging into it heart and soul. Find something you can get excited about and diligently pursue it. If your spirits are low, get involved in something. If you're involved in something, try something else. People rarely succeed at things they can't get excited about.

25. Are you intelligently persistent? Pursue your ideas with insatiable diligence but keep thinking, believing and adapting as you do. Try new approaches to reaching your goals and guard against burning yourself out. As Coleman Cox noted, "Even the woodpecker owes his success to the fact that he uses his head and keeps pecking away until he finishes the job he starts."

26. Have you started working on turning that No. 1 idea of yours into a reality? If not, why not get started now? Both you and the world can be richer for it. If you don't have a No. 1 idea, create one. You now know how. Walt Disney, one of the greatest imagineers of all time, summed up his formula for

creative success when he said: "Somehow I can't believe that there are any heights that can't be scaled by a man who knows the secret of making dreams come true. This special secret, it seems to me, can be summarized in four C's. They are Curiosity, Confidence, Courage and Constancy and the greatest of these is confidence. When you believe in a thing, believe in it all the way, implicitly and unquestionably."

The universe is filled with an infinite number of new ideas patiently waiting to be discovered and turned into wonderful realities. Here's hoping you avail yourself of this invitation to creative success and reap the ecstasies of creative absorption. May the flow be with you.

Index

Piatkus Business Books

Piatkus Business Books have been created for people who need expert knowledge readily available in a clear and easy-to-follow format. All the books are written by specialists in their field. They will help you improve your skills quickly and effortlessly in the workplace and on a personal level.

Titles include:

Brain Power: the 12-week mental training programme Marilyn vos Savant and Leonore Fleischer

The Complete Time Management System Christian H Godefroy and John Clark

How to Win Customers and Keep Them for Life Michael LeBoeuf

Improve Your Profits: practical advice for the small to medium sized business Malcolm Bird

Marketing Yourself: how to sell yourself and get the jobs you've always wanted Dorothy Leeds

Memory Booster: easy techniques for rapid learning and a better memory Robert W Finkel

Powerspeak: the complete guide to public speaking and presentation Dorothy Leeds

Quantum Learning: unleashing the genius in you Bobbi DePorter with Mike Hernacki

Right Brain Manager, The: how to use the power of your mind to achieve personal and professional success Dr Harry Alder

Say What You Mean and Get What You Want George R Walther

Three Minute Meditator, The David Harp with Nina Feldman

Winning New Business: a practical guide to successful sales presentations Dr David Lewis

For a free brochure with further information on our complete range of business titles, please write to:

Piatkus Books
Freepost 7 (WD 4505)
London W1E 4EZ

PIATKUS